WATER POLLUTION

ECONOMIC ASPECTS AND RESEARCH NEEDS

By Allen V. Kneese

PUBLISHED BY RESOURCES FOR THE FUTURE, INC.

Distributed by The Johns Hopkins Press, Baltimore and London

Preface

Public agencies and industry will probably spend tens of billions of dollars on new water pollution abatement facilities in the next few decades. Added billions will be spent for the operation of new and existing facilities. How can physical science research reduce the cost of achieving objectives? And how can social science research make sure that the right objectives are being efficiently pursued?

Such questions are particularly difficult. In a very abstract and formal sense, economic theory provides a criterion for the appropriate level of research outlays. Additional research expenditures should be undertaken if the marginal return from them exceeds the marginal outlay, and they should be continued until the two are brought into equality. Unfortunately, the uncertain productivity of research makes anything like a fully satisfactory forecast of results impossible. Even when the goals are rather clearly defined, the commitment of resources to research activity remains, in considerable measure, an act of faith. However, in the past, these uncertain undertakings have often paid off handsomely, and it is becoming less necessary to rely on "serendipity" and increasingly possible to successfully direct scientific research toward goals of high social value.

Although it is not possible to say precisely how much human and physical capital should be devoted to pollution control research, it appears that the present effort is very small compared with the importance of the field and the potential "payoffs" involved. A recent article on the physical and biological science research effort in the field of water supply and pollution control estimates that $3.5 million from all sources was spent in 1958 in support of water-supply and pollution-control research.[1] The authors estimate that no more than 400 to 450 professionally trained persons are engaged, either full or part time, in water supply and pollution control research in the United States. They conclude that "paucity of research personnel is not the only somber note provided by this analysis. One senses a fragmentation of program,

[1] H. G. Hanson and B. B. Berger, "Where Does Research Stand in Water Pollution Control?" *Journal, Water Pollution Control Federation*, May 1961.

iv

a lack of co-ordination among projects, over-attention to refinements on the one hand and inattention to major problems on the other."

An even greater underallocation of resources exists with respect to the social sciences. Water pollution is in the very fullest sense a social phenomenon and clearly poses difficult questions for economic theory, political science, public administration, social psychology, and other disciplines concerning themselves with social phenomena and public policy. Pollution raises fundamental issues with respect to the character of property rights in resources, the allocation of resources where "spillovers" destroy parity between private and social valuations, the allocation of resources to public or common goods, public decision-making under conditions of uncertainty, and the design of efficient administrative structures as well as the design of efficient physical systems. Nevertheless, the merest handful of social scientists concern themselves to any extent with the issues raised by pollution.

Clearly, water pollution presents a problem of allocating scarce research resources. This means that a careful assessment of problems is required to help provide focus and orientation in a field where multitudinous questions present themselves for investigation.

This monograph is directed to the orientation of the research effort, and the tool used for this purpose is an economic framework. Waste disposal is viewed as a problem in the economic theory of efficient resource allocation. This approach highlights the areas where research is needed to help evaluate the various aspects of the cost of water pollution and to develop improved plans for dealing with pollution problems.

The survey arises out of the general interest of Resources for the Future, Inc., in resources problems and in part is meant to help define the role that RFF itself may play in dealing with present and prospective water pollution. It focuses upon a limited range of issues and does not attempt to address institutional and administrative problems. Emphasis is placed on technical and economic aspects, which are important in their own right and which can help clarify and illuminate the broader set of issues.

ALLEN V. KNEESE

Acknowledgments

Many individuals contributed to this study. Outstanding among them are two of my colleagues at RFF—Irving Fox, Vice President, and John Krutilla, Associate Director of the Water Resources Program, both of whom gave valuable guidance in all stages of planning and execution.

A number of other individuals discussed important elements of the study with me and/or commented on a review draft. These include Siegfried Balke, Minister for Atomic Energy and Water Economics, Federal Republic of Germany; Blair Bower, then with the Meramec Basin Research Project; Francis T. Christy, Jr., Research Associate, RFF; Herbert Clare, Regional Program Director, Water Supply and Pollution Control, U.S. Public Health Service, Region VI; Marion Clawson, Director of the Land Program at RFF; Edward J. Cleary, Executive Director, Ohio River Valley Water Sanitation Commission; Lyle E. Craine, School of Natural Resources, Department of Conservation, University of Michigan; Leonard B. Dworsky, Chief of the Public Health Service Water Supply and Pollution Control Program, Columbia Basin; Rolf Eliassen, Department of Sanitary Engineering, Stanford University; Harold Ellis, Agricultural Research Service; Gordon M. Fair, Department of Sanitary Engineering, Harvard University; L. M. Falkson, Department of Economics, Harvard University; James Flannery, Economist, U.S. Public Health Service; Charles D. Gates, Department of Sanitary Engineering, Cornell University; Karl Gertel, Agricultural Research Service; John Geyer, Department of Sanitary Engineering, Johns Hopkins University; Michael Gucovsky, Conservation Foundation; Eleanor Hanlon, Research Associate, RFF; Orris Herfindahl, Research Associate, RFF; Maynard Hufschmidt, Water Resources Seminar, Harvard University; C. H. J. Hull, Department of Sanitary Engineering, Johns Hopkins University; Edgar Landenberger, U.S. Corps of Engineers; Ray K. Linsley, Executive Head, Department of Civil Engineering, Stanford University; Walter Lynn, Department of Sanitary Engineering, Cornell University; P. H. McGauhey, Director, Sanitary Engineering Laboratory, University of California; Kenneth C. Nobe, Project Economist, Colorado River Basin

Water Quality Control Project, U.S. Public Health Service; Walter L. Picton, Director, Water and Sewerage Industry and Utilities Division, U.S. Department of Commerce; George Reid, Director, Bureau of Water Resources Research, University of Oklahoma; Melvin Scheidt, Program Adviser, Water Requirements Planning, U.S. Public Health Service; Ernest Tsivogolou of the Robert A. Taft Sanitary Engineering Center, U.S. Public Health Service; C. J. Velz, Chairman, Department of Environmental Health, University of Michigan; S. V. Ciriacy-Wantrup, Department of Agricultural Economics, University of California; Lowdon Wingo, Jr., Research Associate, RFF; Nathaniel Wollman, Department of Economics, University of New Mexico; and Abel Wolman, Chairman, Department of Sanitary Engineering, Johns Hopkins University.

While the study was greatly improved by incorporation of reviewers' suggestions, I did not accept all the suggestions offered. Consequently, the listing of an individual's name does not necessarily indicate full concurrence with content or manner of presentation.

A.V.K.

Contents

Contents

Part I

AN ECONOMIC FRAMEWORK

I

Introduction

Some early projections of national water requirements failed to consider that water use ordinarily is not completely consumptive and that residuals are available for further use. In several more recent studies this oversight was corrected, or perhaps even over-corrected. Consumption of water came to be regarded as a physical phenomenon resulting almost entirely from evaporation and transpiration. From the point of view of economics such a definition is inadequate. While evaporation and transpiration are indeed consumptive in that they preclude further uses, other changes resulting from water use may have an analogous effect. It is exclusion or increased cost of alternative uses that constitutes loss or consumption, or better yet, the real cost of water use. Emphasis on losses or costs viewed as foregone opportunities helps to clarify the problem of water resources use and development and helps to tie the analysis into the general framework of an economic allocation theory. It is evident, of course, that changes in water quality resulting from various uses may either foreclose completely or raise the cost of subsequent uses of water, and thus be as clearly consumptive as if an actual transformation from the liquid to the vapor state had occurred.

Most recent, general studies of water resources have given at least a nod to quality problems. However, the first comprehensive projection of water requirements that formally and specifically includes requirements for pollution abatement was recently undertaken by Resources for the Future, with the co-operation of the Senate Select Committee on Water Resources. The study was directed by Dr. Nathaniel Wollman and a report of preliminary findings was published as a print of the Senate Select Committee.[1]

[1] *Water Resources Activities in the United States—Water Supply and Demand,* Select Committee on National Water Resources, United States Senate, Committee Print No. 32 (Washington: U.S. Government Printing Office, August 1960). See also Committee Print No. 29 (July 1960), *Water Requirements for Pollution Abatement* by George W. Reid, from which the estimates of dilution water requirements used in Print 32 were obtained.

1

The report concludes that in most regions—especially in the East—a far larger share of future water supplies must be devoted to providing dilution for industrial and domestic organic wastes than will be consumed by evaporation and transpiration. This result emerged even when high levels of waste treatment were assumed. The conclusions were based upon the assumption that current relationships of wastes produced to population and economic activity would continue, that a rate of 4 ppm of dissolved oxygen was to be maintained in all streams, and that standard biological treatment and augmentation of low stream flows for waste dilution would be the only devices used to deal with pollution loadings. Given these assumptions, the report further concluded that a minimum cost combination of flow augmentation and treatment would require an additional abatement investment of perhaps $100 billion (1954 prices) by the year 2000.

This is indeed a huge sum. By contrast, the cost of completing the Bureau of Reclamation program of multipurpose development is estimated at a mere $4 billion after 1954, and the aggregate of federal appropriations for water resource development from 1824 to 1954 was reported to have been only $14 billion.[2]

Preliminary results of the RFF-Senate Select Committee study cannot be viewed as much more than a broad indicator of the potential magnitude of various aspects of water supply problems. However, they do suggest that future water quality control investment could be larger than any other public investment in natural resources development. Thus it will certainly be highly deserving of the attention of those interested in efficient investment and operating decisions in the resources field. A variety of complexities, a number of which will emerge in the discussion of the following sections, makes efficient and socially meaningful planning for pollution control unusually difficult. The physical sciences, engineering, economics, political science, and public administration must all play a role in dealing with a wide range of complex problems.

Economics can, to a degree, act as a unifying agent and provide guidelines for research in the several fields of study that have an important bearing upon the nation's ability to respond constructively to

[2] Task Force on Water Resources and Power for the Commission on Organization of the Executive Branch of the Government, *Report on Water Resources and Power* (Washington: U.S. Government Printing Office, 1957), p. 6. Since the appropriations for the period 1924-1954 were made at current prices throughout the period, valuation in terms of present prices would raise the amount considerably.

developing pollution problems. For example, projection of economic trends and their implications, especially when done on a regional basis, can be helpful in indicating emerging challenges to technology and management and giving them some dimension. This was a useful result of the Wollman-Senate Select Committee study. The mere fact that such projections may not accurately characterize the actual evolution of events does not mean that they are useless. On the contrary, projections may go astray precisely because the problems they delineate are subsequently dealt with. The high pollution abatement costs projected by the Wollman-Senate Select Committee study may elicit research in sciences and engineering and adjustments in management procedure that will enable society to deal more efficiently with the problem.

Moreover, economic reasoning can provide guidelines for determining both the physical area of a planning unit and the scope of administrative powers. For example, it appears that unified planning over rather extensive geographical areas is necessary for dealing efficiently with pollution in economically developed regions, since water use and waste disposal by one unit can have a direct effect on the operations of others. The notion of externalities or third party effects, which is utilized extensively in succeeding sections and which is comparatively well elaborated in economic theory, sheds considerable light upon the appropriate minimum size of planning units. Such units should be large enough to comprehend or make internal the more significant influences external to individual economic units. Furthermore, economic considerations should help specify the powers of a planning authority. For example, an efficient waste-disposal plan for an area that contains numerous interdependent decision-making units may well imply a distribution of pollution costs not conducive to appropriate allocation of resources. Under these circumstances it may be desirable for the responsible agency to have the power to collect charges and pay bounties, and to finance, construct, and operate abatement works.

The interrelationships of economics and the institutions and administrative arrangements most suitable for the implementation of pollution abatement policy are interesting and highly important. However, their detailed study can best be pursued once the economics of pollution abatement and its place in intelligent social policy are better understood.

In this study waste disposal is viewed as an aspect of economic activity in an economy where the allocation of resources to alternative uses is accomplished primarily by market processes. The special circumstances surrounding waste disposal are recognized as grounds for public intervention and for the insertion of some politically determined values into the processes of public policy formation. The primary purpose is to conceptualize the pollution problem in a way that helps to identify types of physical, economic, and social knowledge that are basic to intelligent policy in the pollution field. Part I is largely devoted to establishing this general framework.

II

Water Pollution – Nature, Effects, Treatment, Alternatives to Treatment

Water pollution results from a great variety of causes, includes complex changes in receiving waters, and affects subsequent water uses in numerous rather subtle, as well as obvious, ways. A full description of the physical aspects of water pollution and the technical devices available for its abatement can easily fill an extensive volume.[1] These matters are summarized here to provide background for discussion of the economics of pollution control policy.

MAJOR POLLUTANTS AND THEIR EFFECTS ON RECEIVING WATERS

Conservative and Nonconservative Pollutants

Pollutants that enter water courses as a result of man's domestic, industrial, and agricultural activities can be grouped in a variety of ways. One very broad division, which emphasizes occurrences within the receiving water, distinguishes between conservative and nonconservative pollutants.

Conservative pollutants are not altered by the biological processes that occur in natural waters. For the most part these are the inorganic chemicals such as chlorides which, once they enter the receiving water, are diluted but not appreciably changed in quantity. Industrial wastes contain numerous such pollutants including metallic salts and other toxic, corrosive, colored, and taste-producing materials. Domestic pollution

[1] Good examples are Gordon Maskew Fair and John Charles Geyer, *Water Supply and Waste-Water Disposal* (New York: John Wiley and Sons, Inc., 1956), and Louis Klein, *Aspects of River Pollution* (New York: Academic Press, Inc., 1957).

also contains chlorides and other dissolved salts. Return flow from irrigation carries dissolved solids, predominantly chlorides.

Nonconservative pollutants are substances that are changed in form and/or reduced in quantity by the biological, chemical, and physical phenomena characteristic of natural waters. By far the most widespread source of such materials is domestic sewage. This highly unstable, putrescible, organic waste can be converted to inorganic materials (bicarbonates, nitrates, sulphates, and phosphates) by the bacteria and other organisms typical of natural water bodies.

If water is not too heavily loaded, this process of "self-purification" will proceed aerobically (i.e., by the action of bacteria utilizing free oxygen) and will not produce offensive odors. If, however, the receiving waters are loaded beyond a certain level, the process of biological degradation becomes anaerobic (i.e., proceeds by the action of bacteria not utilizing free oxygen), and noxious hydrogen sulfide gas as well as methane and other gases will be produced.

The aerobic and anaerobic processes, which naturally occur in streams, are utilized in sewage treatment plants and, indeed, are the major elements in ordinary sewage treatment. In essence, treatment plants systematize, control, and accelerate the processes that would have occurred in any case and by so doing can limit the self-purification burden put upon a water body.

Domestic sewage is the most widespread source of degradable organic wastes, but industry contributes about an equal amount. The food and pulp and paper industries are the greatest generators of such wastes, and in some instances individual plants emit massive loads. For example, a single sugar beet processing plant, during its seasonal period of operation, may produce organic wastes equivalent to the sewage flow of a city of half a million people.

BOD, the Oxygen Sag, and Algae

Predicting the concentration of given amounts of conservative pollutants presents no particular difficulty since dilution is essentially the only process involved. However, predicting the level of unassimilated degradable organic wastes, the rate of waste degradation, and important associated variables presents more imposing technical problems.

A measure of organic pollution load is Biochemical Oxygen Demand (BOD), which indicates the rate at which dissolved oxygen is drawn upon in a stream. The rate at which a given quantity and type of organic waste exerts oxygen demand is a function of a variety of factors; among the most important are temperature and chemical characteristics of the receiving water. Toxins, for example, may appreciably reduce the rate of BOD by inhibiting bacterial action. In extreme instances of toxic pollution a body of water may become bacteriologically "dead." Thus a link is established between conservative and nonconservative pollutants. On the other hand, at higher temperatures bacterial action is accelerated, wastes are degraded more rapidly, and dissolved oxygen in the water is drawn upon more heavily. Furthermore, the oxygen saturation level of warm water is lower than that of cooler water. Thus increased temperatures tend to squeeze dissolved oxygen levels in waste receiving waters, conceivably to the point of producing septic (anaerobic) conditions. Warmer water—as well as typically low stream flows—tends to make summer the critical period for organic pollution. Moreover, it is in part because of its effect on the oxygen balance that heated water can be considered a pollutant.[2]

The rate of BOD combined with the rate at which oxygen is restored determines the level of dissolved oxygen. In flowing water the combined effect of BOD and reaeration results first in a fall and then in a rise in dissolved oxygen as the wastes are carried downstream. This phenomenon is described by a characteristic curve known as the oxygen sag. The low, or critical, point on the oxygen sag is the focus of attention when sewage treatment plants are designed. Other things being equal, factors that reduce the rate at which BOD is exerted lengthen and flatten the oxygen sag, while accelerated BOD has the reverse effect. The shape of the oxygen sag is also affected by other factors such as the velocity of stream flow and the rate of reaeration, which depends largely on turbulence, the area of the air-water interface relative to volume, and photosynthetic oxygen production.

Actually BOD proceeds in two distinct stages. If an untreated waste is put in a clean stream, a first and major draft upon dissolved oxygen occurs as the putrescible wastes are degraded by bacterial action. Thereafter the dissolved oxygen level tends to recover. Farther downstream, roughly five to seven days travel time, a "second stage" BOD occurs as the nitrogen embodied in organic sewage is converted to nitrite and to nitrate by aerobic "nitrifying" bacteria. The "second stage" BOD tends to be more diffuse and does not tend to carry dissolved oxygen to as low a level as does the first stage BOD.

[2] It, of course, also lessens the efficiency of the receiving water as a cooling medium.

Both the degradation of putrescible wastes and the process of nitrification can be carried on in a treatment plant rather than in the receiving water. However, orthodox treatment measures do not fully complete either process and so the water's self-purification capacity is always called upon to a degree.

The residual products of organic waste degradation are plant nutrients (nitrogen, phosphorus, carbon), which may give rise to algae growth in the receiving water. Since algae produce organic matter by means of photosynthesis, they periodically release oxygen and affect the oxygen balance of the receiving water. If algae occur in great quantities they affect the appearance, taste, and odor of water.

Persistent Organics and Radiological Pollution

A very large number of organic compounds have been synthesized by the chemical industry. Most of these—while not strictly conservative pollutants—are to some degree resistant to attack by stream biota. Consequently they are often called the "persistent" organics. Since biota found in streams are also the ones typically utilized in waste treatment, the synthetic organics have proved resistant to treatment. Some of the organic chemicals found in streams at least intermittently are comparatively common, for example, DDT, 2,4-D, chlordane, cyanides and synthetic detergents; many others are complex industrial, agricultural, and pharmaceutical chemicals. In addition to presenting difficult treatment problems, the agricultural chemicals are often delivered to streams in storm runoff from the land and hence are not accessible to waste-treatment plants.

Radiological pollution is somewhat in the same class as the "persistent" organics with respect to the conservative-nonconservative classification. All radioactive elements are in the process of decay but in some instances the process is so slow that they must be considered among the conservative pollutants. Presently, radioactive waste discharge, because of its rather extreme implications for public health, is strictly limited.

Bacterial Pollution

Bacterial pollution, along with the degradable organics, has been the major focus of pollution control policy. The "coliform count" is a traditional measure of sewage pollution. Actually the coliform count is only useful for indicator or index purposes. The real source of concern is the bacteria that cause infectious diseases—primarily typhoid, dysentery, and cholera. These bacteria may be considered nonconservative pollutants since they tend to die off rather quickly after leaving the body. Thus a stream is capable of purifying itself of such bacteria in the course of its flow.

The presence of viruses in sewage and in watercourses has recently drawn much attention. Several common varieties of viruses are more resistant to disinfectants than pathogenic bacteria and are more viable outside the human body environment.

Sediment Pollution

One type of pollution, which is of major significance in some basins, results from land erosion. Suspended sediment might be considered a conservative pollutant in the sense that it is not subject to changing form, since it is largely inorganic in character. However, since it is in suspension rather than in solution, there is a tendency for it to settle out —especially in slow stretches of stream or in impoundments. Turbidity, which may be caused by suspended sediment, is involved with other aspects of the condition of water bodies. For example, algae growth, being dependent upon light, is associated with the clarity of water.[3]

Concluding Comments

The above discussion has perhaps served to illustrate that while a simple classification system is a convenient point of departure, it must inevitably obscure the highly complex phenomena that occur in a stream. A vast number of substances enter watercourses, some resulting from man's activities and others being of natural origin, and they are interrelated in a variety of complicated ways.

Natural lakes, reservoirs, and tidal estuaries present even more difficult problems for analysis than flowing streams. Deposition of sludge banks, with the possibility of their sudden dispersal resulting in a pollution "shock load," is one complication characteristic of quiescent waters. Plant nutrients take on special significance in lakes and reservoirs because they tend to accumulate over time and contribute to depletion of oxygen in the lower levels of such water bodies. In tidal

[3] If turbidity is caused by colloidal matter, it will not settle out. Domestic sewage and industrial trade wastes usually contain turbidity-causing colloidal material.

estuaries, wastes may be carried back and forth within the estuary for long periods of time rather than disperse into the ocean. Thus unassimilated or partially assimilated wastes may build up in estuarine areas and become particularly troublesome.

EFFECTS OF POLLUTION ON WATER USES

Aesthetic and Recreational Considerations

The earliest efforts to control pollution had their origin in man's aesthetic sensitivities. The repulsive suffocating reek of large cities of early modern times is made plain in many accounts. The smells so graphically described were largely the result of the anaerobic processes mentioned earlier. So long as sewers are covered and receiving waters are not in a septic (anaerobic) state, odor problems are likely to be minimal. Nuisance odors can be largely eliminated by satisfactorily designed sewers conveying wastes to an adequate supply of dilution water, but the early sewers often served merely to concentrate the odor-producing processes in the neighborhood of outfalls.

Aesthetically repulsive conditions are not limited to those offending the sense of smell. Floating material of any kind is likely to be offensive, and floating sewage solids especially so. Suspended sediment and industrial wastes, including dyes, also reduce the visual appeal of water. Dense algae growth resulting from large supplies of sewage residual plant nutrients makes water both unattractive and odorous.

The rewards of water-based recreation are certainly related to the aesthetic qualities of water, but the recreational value of water can be reduced or eliminated by pollution which does not render the water repulsive nor even necessarily unattractive. For example, the organic waste load in a stream may reduce dissolved oxygen (D.O.) levels to a point where the best quality fish are unable to survive, or toxins from industrial plants or agricultural lands may kill fish directly, interfere with a phase of their life cycle, or affect a necessary food source. Higher temperatures, excessive acidity or alkalinity and low D.O., all of which can result from man-made pollution, increase the sensitivity of fish to toxins and in extreme instances can kill fish. On the other hand, a modest degree of sewage pollution can be beneficial to fishing waters because of the increased algae growth that enters into the food chain. Extensive growths, however, can be toxic to fish. A special problem occurs in reservoirs where algae growth and decay combined with "stratification" of the reservoir (i.e., absence of deep circulation) cause its deeper parts to become devoid of dissolved oxygen and, consequently, to become uninhabitable for fish.

The effect of pollution on bathing also extends beyond aesthetic considerations. Water that is otherwise attractive might be deemed unsafe for swimming because of its bacterial count.

Domestic Supplies

Pollution also presents obstacles to obtaining high quality water supplies for domestic purposes. The amount and character of treatment required is related to the quality of intake water. Water containing organic substances that are only partly assimilated requires larger amounts of chlorination to achieve the free chlorine residual necessary to kill bacteria. Corrosive, saline, or hard waters produce undesirable effects by corroding equipment, requiring special installations in homes or commercial establishments, requiring large quantities of soap, inducing purchase of bottled water, and necessitating additional treatment of public supplies.

Furthermore, water is made less palatable by certain pollutants. Algae growth may cause unattractive tastes and odors, and large amounts of algae in intake water increase treatment problems. A great variety of chemicals of industrial origin affect the palatability and possibly the safety of water supplies; they may require special treatment or may even make a water supply completely unsuitable for domestic use. Furthermore, the appearance of water may be made less suitable by industrial and domestic pollution. For example, color is undesirable in drinking water as is the foaming which results from even minute concentrations of detergents.

Industrial Supplies

Many industrial processes utilize a quality of water not unlike that usually prepared by municipal treatment plants. However, the range of qualities required or desirable in industrial application is very wide. Cooling water can often be of comparatively low sanitary quality, but the presence of heat and of corrosive and scale-forming materials is undesirable. Some processes require unusually soft water; others need comparatively hard water. A large part of the water used in the paper and pulp industry can be of relatively low quality in some respects, but it should contain little iron, manganese, and carbon dioxide. High-pressure boiler feed water, used in a variety of industries, must be of very high quality to prevent corrosion, scale formation, and the accumulation of biological slimes. Steel rolling mills are damaged by water containing concentrations of chlorides tolerable in drinking water.

Pollution Establishes a Technical Link Between Economic Units

By affecting, in a variety of ways, activities dependent upon water quality, pollution establishes a *technical* link between economic (industrial, commercial, and household) units. Thus the level at which one economic unit carries on its activities is not independent of the range and character of opportunities of other economic units. As will be elaborated at a later point, independence of economic units is an essential element in producing the desirable results often attributed to the operation of free markets. Consequently, an essential element of the pollution "problem" is that the damages of waste disposal into water courses are in most instances external to the polluting unit (industrial plant, mine, municipality, or firm, for example).

METHODS OF TREATMENT AND SOME ALTERNATIVES

The Range of Alternatives

Given the quantity of wastes, the quality of water bodies can in general be altered in a desirable way either by treating the wastes or by increasing dilution. As long as dilution water can be made available and the focus is upon maintenance of quality during low-flow periods, waste treatment and dilution can be viewed as technical substitutes.[4] Enhanced dilution can be attained either by altering the time pattern of stream flows or by altering the time pattern of waste discharge.

Given the degree of dilution, water supply treatment can be a partial substitute for sewage treatment. Indeed, if water were not useful, offensive, or altered in quality while *in situ,* water supply treatment would—technically—be completely interchangeable with sewage treatment.

[4] If floating materials are involved, a degree of treatment (i.e., screening out solids and disposing of them) must take place before dilution can achieve the same results as normal treatment.

Process changes in industry which recover, reclaim, or otherwise reduce waste loads, as well as changes in the character of products and disposal on the land surface, are also, within limits, alternatives to treatment.

A system best designed to achieve social objectives in, say, a river basin would probably incorporate a variety of measures including water-supply treatment, sewage treatment, augmented dilution flows, process changes, co-ordination of effluent releases with river flow, and perhaps others. The idea of an optimal system of waste disposal is elaborated in the following sections. In the next few pages a brief outline of the general character of the major available water quality control measures is presented. A primary point to be made is that the limit upon society's ability to avoid water pollution is not technical. Technically (disregarding costs), measures can be instituted to produce water of any desired quality.

Treatment

Sewage. Completely pure water could be obtained from sewage effluent by a series of treatment measures including careful distillation. At the present time, however, orthodox treatment of domestic wastes is a comparatively standardized process that can greatly reduce but not eliminate BOD and that is frequently designed to improve bacteriological quality. Industrial waste treatment is generally similar but, in some cases, additional techniques are used for treating color, adjusting acidity, or alkalinity (by neutralization), or reducing the concentration of various chemicals (primarily by precipitation or ion exchange).

Ordinarily the treatment of degradable organic wastes begins with removal of the larger solids by screening and the more finely divided ones by sedimentation. This stage is known as primary treatment. A wet, difficult to handle, sludge results from primary treatment and is ordinarily digested in heated anaerobic tanks before final disposal. However, other sludge disposal techniques, including partial or complete drying and incineration, are also utilized. The burning of wet sludge has recently attracted attention. In many instances, primary treatment, with sludge disposal, is all that is given an effluent containing organic wastes. When this is the case, first stage BOD is reduced by perhaps 40 per cent.

A further, or secondary, stage of treatment is biological in character and essentially controls and accelerates the self-purification processes that occur in natural waters. Two major techniques are presently used —one incorporates a "trickling filter" and the other an "activated sludge plant." When secondary treatment is undertaken, the supernatant liquor from the sludge digestor (or other liquid resulting from the handling of sludge) is routed through the process. Secondary treatment in turn gives rise to some additional sludge which is routed into the digestors. Primary plus secondary treatment is capable of reducing BOD by some 85-95 per cent. Chlorine is sometimes added to effluent from treatment plants, primarily to kill bacteria. The essential elements of the primary-secondary treatment sequence have been unchanged for more than forty years.

During secondary treatment a process of "nitrification" may occur. This means that the organic nitrogen content of the sewage is successively converted to organic nitrogen, nitrites, and nitrates. Over all, the volume of potential plant nutrients (nitrogen and phosphorous) is reduced moderately during secondary treatment, but the content of nitrates rises if nitrification occurs. Within limits, the extent to which nitrification occurs in the treatment plant, rather than in the receiving water, can be controlled.

When a particularly high-quality effluent is desired, or when a seasonal or an unusually difficult treatment problem exists, the components or combinations of components in the treatment sequence may be altered. For example, chemical precipitation may be used to deal with seasonal or other specialized treatment problems, especially industrial ones. By means of precipitation and flocculation, much of the suspended matter and some dissolved solids can be settled out of water containing organic wastes. A device sometimes used to improve final effluent, especially from small treatment plants, is a finishing pond. This is an aerobic lagoon in which biological processes are permitted to continue before the effluent is finally expelled into the receiving water.

Similar types of ponds are increasingly used as complete or secondary treatment devices. In such "oxidation" ponds, heavy algae growth furnishes—by means of photosynthesis—a substantial share of the oxygen requirements of aerobic bacteria. While highly consumptive of space, such ponds are, when properly designed and loaded, capable of stabilizing oxygen-demanding wastes to a high degree.

If fish or algae are harvested from oxidation ponds,[5] the process of

[5] At the present time fish are harvested in a few locations in Europe and Asia. Algae have been harvested only on an experimental basis.

biological purification is accelerated and a major portion of the plant nutrients can be removed. To a degree, other chemicals are also extracted from the waste water. High-rate oxidation ponds and related "tertiary" treatment methods for plant nutrients are presently in an experimental stage.

Water Supply. Public water-supply treatment typically incorporates some of the same steps as sewage treatment. Technically all the steps involved in sewage treatment could be performed at the water-treatment plant, or repeated there. In the United States, sewage effluent has been recirculated for municipal supplies only under conditions of extreme stringency. In the few instances where this was done, water treatment was essentially an extension of sewage treatment.

In practice, the treatment of water from a surface source often begins with coagulation (analogous to the flocculation described in connection with sewage treatment) followed by sedimentation. A further process is filtration through sand, which clarifies the water and removes substantial numbers of bacteria. The removal of iron and manganese, if the water source is ground water, and water softening may be included among the treatment processes. Other treatments to reduce corrosiveness and tastes and odors are frequently included, at least periodically. These commonly are accomplished by the application of lime and activated carbon. Finally, chlorine is usually added to the water to destroy harmful organisms; the amount required is, among other things, a function of the unstabilized organic content of the water.

Industrial water-supply treatment typically includes some or all of the same steps. Quality requirements vary widely, however, and large amounts of industrial water can be treated by methods unsuitable for potable supplies. Manufacturers may harden or soften water, adjust its alkalinity or acidity, and remove undesirable chemical substances of various kinds. In uses where extremely high quality is critical, water may be demineralized or distilled prior to use.

Dilution

Dilution of wastes beyond that provided by natural flow during low-flow periods can be provided in two ways. The pattern of streamflow may be changed or the pattern of waste discharge into the stream may be altered. The former conceivably could be done by several means but the most common is low-flow augmentation by means of controlled release from reservoir storage. The latter can be accomplished by temporary storage of wastes for release during periods of increased streamflow or by the temporary shutdown of polluting industrial plants during low stream stages.

The dependence of pollution levels on streamflow establishes close links between pollution abatement and other aspects of multipurpose flow-control projects in a basin. For example, flow control for navigation in some instances is complementary with flow augmentation for waste dilution (i.e., it is accomplished by the same water and storage space). But waste dilution is ordinarily competitive with irrigation. Use of power dams for peaking produces sharp variations in flow, which bear upon the desirability of temporary storage of wastes. Many interdependencies of analogous character are possible. Consequently, pollution control is an integral part of multipurpose water resources development. Efficient water resources development cannot occur without identification and evaluation of significant interdependencies.

Other Measures

Wastes can, of course, be disposed of by methods which do not permit them to enter water courses. Irrigation with sewage effluents is a venerable measure of this character, as are various means of disposing of domestic wastes in a more or less dry state.

Where public water supply standards are the primary consideration, alternative sources of supply can technically be substituted for sewage treatment and water-supply treatment. This might involve transportation of surface supplies, tapping of ground-water supplies, and/or artificial recharge of ground waters.

CONCLUDING COMMENTS

This discussion has greatly simplified many aspects of water quality control and completely neglected others. One point, however, is clear. Technically, a great variety of alternative measures are available for quality control. These can be made to substitute for one another in various ways and at various rates depending upon circumstances and upon the particular pollutants under consideration. Furthermore, it is clear that decisions concerning the proper extent of application and proper balance among control measures cannot be rationally made on technical grounds alone. Accordingly, values must be introduced into the decision-making process.

The U.S. economy generally depends upon private enterprise and market processes for the generation of values and on private decisions to incorporate them into the economic decision-making process in an efficient fashion. For a variety of reasons, unregulated market processes cannot deal efficiently with pollution. Consequently, there are adequate grounds for public intervention and planning in this area, even though the general rationale for a market economy is accepted. Indeed, in large measure, such intervention can be justified by the desirability of moving actual results more closely into line with ideal market results. Further, there are grounds for considering values not arising from market-type valuation at all. The next chapter is addressed to an elaboration of these points.

III

Economic Efficiency, Social Policy, and the Pollution Problem

THE "WELFARE MAXIMIZING" RESULTS OF MARKET PROCESSES

There is something approaching a consensus among economists that a well-functioning market system is an efficient device for allocating resources in correspondence with consumer wants.[1] If markets are highly competitive and consumers and producers are rationally attempting to achieve the greatest possible benefit for themselves, the available resources will be allocated in a way that maximizes economic welfare.

In such an economy each productive resource will be used up to the point where the cost of an additional unit is just equal to its contribution to the value of production. For example, in the case of labor, additional workers will be hired until the wage paid to the last worker employed just equals the dollar value of the extra product he produces. This will be done because each worker hired up to that point will have added more to the revenues of the firm than to its costs. Now if this condition prevails in each firm and if the price of a resource—say labor—is uniform as between any two firms, the value of product contributed by the last unit of labor used in each firm will be identical. Thus, if the wage for a given quality of labor is uniform for the economy, the value of the product of the last unit hired in any particular line of activity will be equal to that of the last unit hired in any other activity. This is important because it means that the market price paid for a resource represents the product which the resource

[1] No attempt is made here to set out the theory underlying this judgment in extensive detail. For an excellent exposition, see John V. Krutilla and Otto Eckstein, *Multiple Purpose River Development: Studies in Applied Economic Analysis* (Baltimore: Johns Hopkins Press, 1958), Chapter II.

could have generated in another line of activity. For example, if a firm hires an additional unit of labor for one dollar, it means that production elsewhere has been reduced to the extent of one dollar by the withdrawal of that unit of labor. As the "welfare economist" puts it, the market price of the resource is equal to its opportunity cost.

Furthermore, consumers attempting to achieve maximum satisfaction from a given amount of income, will tend to allocate their expenditures in such a way that the last dollar spent for any particular item will yield an amount of satisfaction equal to the last dollar spent on any other item. When this condition exists, it follows that the market price of a particular commodity reflects its worth, or goodness, or want-satisfying power. If the price of one commodity is twice as high per unit as the price of another commodity, the last unit of the higher-priced commodity which an individual buys must yield twice as much satisfaction to him as the last unit of the lower-priced one which he buys. Consequently the relative market prices of goods reflect the valuation which consumers place upon the purchase of marginal units.

If, in addition, the distribution of purchasing power conforms to the ethical standards of the community and if consumer sovereignty over resource allocation is accepted, the prices of goods and factors of production accurately represent their contributions to social welfare. Consequently prices provide automatic, socially valid guidelines for investment and production. For example, presume that a dollar's worth (opportunity cost) of labor can be moved from an activity where it yields a dollar's worth (marginal social value) of product to another activity where, for some reason, labor has not been utilized to the point where the cost of the last unit is equal to the value of product it produces. In the latter activity an additional dollar's worth of labor will thus give rise to more than a dollar's worth of product. Not only does private benefit maximization indicate and induce a shift of labor under these circumstances, but when the shift is made the total value of production is enhanced and total satisfaction derived by society from its use of resources is increased.

In highly idealized form these notions provide a social justification for market processes and a justification for public intervention in those instances where an obstruction of some type prevents private market processes from equating marginal social costs and benefits. The benefit-cost analysis of public water resources projects, for example, proceeds on the basis that prices in private markets generally register social values (opportunity costs and marginal social benefits), but that the market mechanism cannot function adequately to produce optimum water resources development.[2]

It is clear from the above brief sketch that an essential condition for ideal market results is that technical conditions of production and consumption must be such that the full costs and benefits of performing a given act fall upon the unit performing it. If some costs can be shifted to other units, the private costs incurred do not correspond to the full cost to society, and resource allocation is distorted even though markets function in an otherwise ideal fashion. Should, for example, the employment of a mother result in the delinquency of her children, private costs of the employer (i.e. the wage) would not equal social costs. The latter might include such things as property damages, extra police, etc. Indirect effects of this character are variously called "spill-over effects," "third party effects," or more traditionally, "external diseconomies."

While such effects occur in numerous ways in the economy, they are generally felt to be insufficient to negate the normative qualities of free markets. In specific areas, however, spillover effects are significant and require correction via public policy.

MARKET PROCESSES AND WATER POLLUTION

Some of the ways in which water pollution establishes technical links between economic units in heavily populated and industrialized areas have been reviewed in the previous chapter. In most instances the physical character of waste disposal into water courses is such that virtually the entire resulting damages and attendant costs are external to the unit actually discharging the wastes. Consequently, divergences between private and social costs arise, full social marginal costs are not considered in making private decisions, and various departures from ideal resource allocation occur.

Several interrelated types of distortion, which tend to result from unregulated waste disposal, can be readily identified. In the first place, the costs of some economic units are understated (apparently costless waste disposal) and some are overstated (imposed damages and treatment

---

[2] To simplify the actual procedure somewhat, this permits market prices of inputs and outputs to be taken as indicators of opportunity costs and of benefits respectively. Planning is then carried out in such a way as to maximize net benefits realizable from development of the water resource.

costs) relative to social (opportunity) costs. This tends to induce over-production and -consumption of some items and under-production and -consumption of others.

A further distortion occurs because there is excessive waste disposal into receiving waters. Since depositing materials in the receiving waters is apparently costless, less effort is made to recover materials from waste water and to design and operate processes in such a way as to conserve materials, than if the full social costs of disposal were met.

Moreover, a social cost is imposed and resource allocation is distorted by the fact that market processes tend to generate inefficient combinations of water treatment, sewage treatment, and other abatement devices. Two factors operate to produce this result. Since the deposition of wastes into water courses is apparently costless, there exists a systematic bias unfavorable to sewage treatment and other measures for reducing waste loads and favorable to water supply treatment. In addition, measures such as flow augmentation are not usually provided by private enterprises, since polluters and water users cannot be effectively excluded from sharing in the benefits, whether they contribute to the cost or not.

A BASIN-WIDE FIRM

These distortions of ideal market results can perhaps be clarified by imagining a situation in which they would tend not to exist. One way of doing this is to assume that a single firm carries out all water-related activities within a heavily populated and extensively industrialized basin that empties into the ocean. Assume that the firm conducts all water-using industrial enterprises, all water and sewerage utilities (no privately-owned septic tanks, water softeners, etc.), and all water transportation and related facilities, and that the amount of waste generated in the basin is a straightforward function of population and the level of output of particular products.[3] Assume further that the firm

---

[3] It is assumed that all pollution damages are internal to the firm. In the case of water-using industrial enterprises, this is implied by the firm's ownership and operation. In the case of municipal supplies, any damages in pipes, valves, etc., are internal to the firm but damages to water heaters, interior plumbing, etc., ordinarily would not be. Since the objective of the example is to make waste disposal a matter of the internal economics of the firm, it must be assumed that these facilities belong to the firm.

operates all hydroelectric facilities, owns all land and structures in the flood plain, and is the sole provider of flow regulation. Finally, assume that the firm operates in markets which are either competitive or in which public regulatory authorities set prices equal to necessary marginal costs at a level which clears the market. Needless to say, this image is evoked strictly for expository and illustrative purposes. It is not implied that such a firm should or could exist in the U.S. economy.

For the hypothetical firm the problem of basin-wide water resources management becomes a matter of internal economics. Thus, even though there are numerous water-using industries, flow-control structures, etc., in the basin, they are all subject to a single management.

It is interesting and instructive to deduce the way in which such a firm would handle disposal of wastes in order to *maximize its profits* (or, if appropriate, minimize its losses). Actually the relevant analysis is closely analogous to that sketched above with respect to the hiring of labor. The firm would select the combination of water-quality control measures (water-supply treatment, sewage treatment, flow augmentation, co-ordinated releases, etc.) and pollution damages that would minimize the over-all costs associated with waste disposal at its most profitable level and distribution of activities. This would be accomplished by equating the incremental or marginal costs related to waste disposal for all alternatives. For example, if sewage treatment and pollution damages (corrosion, hardness, reduced cooling efficiency, etc.) were the only alternatives, the firm would operate so as to equate marginal treatment costs with the reduction in marginal residual damages. If it did not, there would be an opportunity to reduce over-all costs by shifting between the alternatives.

It is worth noting again that the firm's general objective is actually to maximize profits, but that this implies that costs associated with waste disposal will be minimized at the level and distribution of output corresponding to maximum profits. If, for example, the firm could lower its costs by doing a little less sewage treatment and permitting a little more pollution damage, or by doing a little more water treatment and a little less recovery of wastes, its over-all profit position could not be at a maximum. This point is worth stressing because the idea of minimizing costs associated with waste disposal (damages or costs imposed in the use or distribution of water being among them), and the role of such cost minimization in getting the most benefit from available resources, is called upon repeatedly at later points in this study.

As part of its general profit-maximizing activities, the firm would integrate its pollution control activities with other aspects of its water-related operations. Thus, in computing the costs of alternative quality control devices, it would consider complementary and competitive relationships between different water uses. Accordingly, flow-augmentation costs would have to be determined in light of the fact that this alternative is complementary with navigation, for example, and to a degree with flood control, but at least partly competitive with irrigation. Moreover, the firm would consider the full marginal costs of producing particular products including the costs imposed on other activities by waste disposal.

At this point it may be useful to indicate that the cost-minimizing activities attributed to the firm would, if done in a completely accurate fashion, require a vast amount of information and advanced computational techniques. The specific nature of these complexities will become clearer in subsequent chapters. On the other hand, the major gains realizable from viewing the waste-disposal problem in a comprehensive manner might be comparatively simply realized.

Several interesting results follow from general reasoning concerning waste disposal by the hypothetical firm. In the first place, consideration of the full costs of production would tend to have two sorts of effects: (1) a somewhat different configuration of output, and (2) if we relax the assumption that the amount of waste generated is rigidly determined by output, a reduction in the over-all amount of waste generated below the level that would exist if many independent economic units operated in the basin.[4] It is quite possible, and even likely, however, that the firm would permit some amount of pollution, even though it considered the full costs of waste disposal and instituted a system which minimized costs. Two factors are relevant here. First, equalization of the marginal costs associated with waste disposal in all directions would probably require that some residual pollution damage be permitted and, second, that water supply treatment be to some extent substituted for pollution abatement. An equally significant point, however, is that there would tend to be less pollution than if numerous independent units were operating in the basin.

If markets adequately registered the population's evaluation of all goods and services bought and sold by the hypothetical firm, its solution

---

[4] A smaller unit would compare waste recovery costs with the value of the recovered wastes. The basin-wide firm would compare costs with the value of the recovered material plus pollution damages avoided. Analogous calculations would be made with respect to product and process changes. Thus the larger unit would use the resources available to it more efficiently.

to the waste-disposal problem would be "efficient," as that term is understood in economic welfare theory. Consequently, it might be assumed that the appropriate public policy toward pollution problems could be inferred directly from the actions of a firm so situated that it bears all waste-disposal costs. It is true that such reasoning helps to establish some points relevant to the determination of appropriate public policy. It is clear, for example, that public policy which explicitly recognizes an area (say, a basin) as an interdependent system (as the hypothetical firm would do) would tend to produce results differing in various beneficial ways from those yielded by the operation of free markets in a basin with independent waste-generating and water-using units. Moreover, it becomes apparent that two interrelated problems confront public policy. One is the problem of devising an optimum system for pollution control and water treatment; the other is providing for an appropriate distribution of costs among economic units and activities.[5] Both problems are matters of public concern. Neither is solved by the unregulated operation of markets.

Unfortunately, the acceptance of market results implied in the example of the basin-wide firm is to some extent unjustified. There are reasons to believe that some significant social values with respect to pollution are not (or not adequately) reflected by consumer preferences as expressed in markets for goods and services. Consequently, the explicit recognition of technological links between economic units in the manner of the hypothetical firm, while a very important part of public policy, is not a complete basis for it.

SOCIAL VALUES

The hypothetical basin-wide firm conducts itself differently in regard to waste disposal than would numerous individual units, because it recognizes that the water-related productive activities conducted at one place are technically linked to the range and character of opportunities elsewhere. In deciding upon its output and investment, however, the firm accepts the valuations of individual consumers as expressed in the

---

[5] In order to make sure that the amount of waste generated is "optimum" in, say, a basin, it would be necessary for costs associated with waste disposal to be so distributed that each polluter would bear the full cost of creating an increment of waste. See the discussion by E. A. Renshaw, "Economics of Pollution Control," *Sewage and Industrial Wastes,* Vol. 30, May 1958.

market. Under ordinary conditions this would be in accordance with, indeed required by, efficient resource allocation. However, in some particulars, pollution tends to distort the correspondence between rational individual consumption decisions and welfare maximization.

The reasons are closely analogous to those that account for distortions in production. Technical interdependency (analogous to upstream waste disposal causing damages downstream) and common services (analogous to restraint on the provision of flow augmentation where a private firm cannot successfully impose charges on the beneficiaries) destroy full equivalence between individual and social welfare maximization.[6] Consequently, while public policy can rely on market demand to establish legitimate indicators of the social value of most goods and services affected by pollution-caused interdependencies, it must make special provision for some others with respect to which markets function inadequately. A further elaboration of the basin-wide firm example can help clarify this point.

Commonality in Consumption—The General Environment

The deleterious effects that water pollution can have on the general environment are obvious. Obnoxious odors of septic sewage may carry for miles, and untreated sewage contains materials that will float on and become suspended in water, destroying its beauty. The profit-maximizing, basin-wide firm would not give adequate attention to these aspects of quality in water bodies to which the public is exposed in the course of its everyday activities. The reason is that participation in the aesthetic enjoyment of such waters cannot be parcelled out and sold. Individuals in the community participate in the benefits provided by the aesthetic qualities of contiguous bodies of water whether they help meet the costs of providing and maintaining them or not. There is, therefore, an incentive for each person, acting as an individual, to avoid sharing in the costs. Consequently, a market for the control of

---

[6] Perhaps a third category of distortions, consisting of interdependency between consumption and production, should be included. For example, if water-based recreation is so revivifying that it has a significant effect on productivity, it may be worthwhile for the basin-wide firm to provide recreational facilities beyond the level at which they would be freely bought by consumers. Except with respect to public health in situations where sanitary standards for drinking water are very low, interdependency of this type appears likely to be minor or, at least, very difficult to identify.

the general environmental effects of pollution cannot develop and the firm will not be induced to include the benefits of this "common" or "public" service in its calculations.

When a situation of this character arises, market results must be amended in some fashion by *public* policy if maximum public benefit is to be obtained from water resources. In the basin operated by the hypothetical firm the problem might not arise because cost minimization might incidentally yield aesthetically satisfactory conditions. If it did not, the citizenry of the basin would have to act politically in order to implement its desires. One possible way of doing this would be to select a committee to devise a variety of proposals to be submitted to referendum. Essential elements of these proposals would be a description of their effects and the attendant costs. The desired aesthetic qualities could then be achieved by placing limits or constraints upon the cost-minimizing activities of the firm. The firm would still minimize costs as outlined earlier but it would do so subject to the condition that, say, there were no floating substances on the streams and that aerobic conditions be maintained at all times. Needless to say, the combination of measures that would minimize costs under the constraints (or politically imposed minimum standards) would not necessarily be the same as the one which minimized costs without the constraints. The cost to society for maintaining the aesthetically desirable results would be the difference between the minimum cost of waste disposal yielded by an optimum system without the aesthetic quality standards or constraints and that yielded by an optimum system with the constraints. The citizens of the basin might be willing to impose this cost upon themselves.

Water-based recreation (fishing, bathing, boating, picnicking) might or might not be adequately provided for by the hypothetical firm. If the firm could control access to recreational opportunities in the basin, it would continue to abate the relevant kinds of pollution until the marginal cost of such abatement equalled the value of the recreational opportunity provided.[7] If the firm did not do this it would be minimizing its costs associated with waste disposal, since the foregone opportunities for obtaining revenue from recreation are one such cost.

If the firm were not able to control access, the provision of recreation opportunities would fall into the same category as environmental

---

[7] Plus the marginal value of other benefits flowing from the abatement. The assumption is continued that markets are competitive or that a public authority sets prices which equate demand and marginal cost.

to avoid costs, and some form of collective choice would have to be qualities. Again there would be a universal incentive for individuals substituted for the market process. If administrative costs of controlling access were high relative to the marginal cost of providing recreation opportunities, welfare could be improved by providing recreation without charge and covering costs by some other means.

Interdependency and Indivisibilities in
Public Water Supplies and Public Health

Interdependency in consumption may provide another reason for social rejection of market results. When interdependency exists, consumption of one individual or household is not independent of the benefits achieved by others. Consequently, the satisfactions of different individuals are not simply additive but interrelated in a complex way. For example, there is a community benefit in addition to the individual benefit when an individual consumes a good or service which tends to reduce communicable disease. For this reason, determination of the value of preventive action cannot reasonably be left to market processes.

An additional problem of social choice arises with respect to public water supplies generally. This results from the impracticability of tailoring the quality of public water supply to the individual desires of specific consumers. Economies of scale in the production and distribution of a standard quality are such that the costs of separately controlling quality for each individual household are prohibitive. It is of course possible to tailor water quality to the preferences of individual households by means of expensive home treatment (softening, for example) and the purchase of bottled water. However, public water supply as such is a standard commodity delivered to each consumer regardless of his individual preferences. Thus it becomes necessary to decide upon a generally acceptable quality of water and a political method for expressing social choice is implied. Here, as with respect to environmental effects, rational social choice would depend upon knowledge of effects (probabilities of various diseases, toxicological effects, and damages) corresponding to various costs. Social decision concerning public water supply standards might have the effect of further constraining or limiting the cost minimization objective of the hypothetical basin-wide firm and altering the character of its optimal waste-disposal system.

CONCLUDING COMMENT

The objective of this chapter has been to delineate, in broad terms, the ways in which unregulated market results with respect to water pollution fail to coincide with the requirements of an ideally functioning market system. The example of a hypothetical basin-wide firm, which recognizes that pollution causes technological links between various activities, has been used to help illustrate some of the directions that appropriate public policy might take. Further, it has been pointed out that in regard to some aspects of water quality, interdependency in consumption and conditions of supply are such that individual market valuations either do not exist or do not yield the appropriate social valuations. For these instances, political valuations are implied in a democratic system. None of these considerations in any way negates the general rationale of a competitive market system. Rather they grow out of it.

In the next chapter a general framework for approaching economic aspects of public pollution policy—incorporating the concepts developed in this chapter—is outlined.

IV

Evaluation – Determination and Integration of Individual and Social Values – Focus of Public Policy

THE SOCIAL OBJECTIVE OF WASTE WATER DISPOSAL POLICY

In the previous chapter the idea of a profit-maximizing, basin-wide firm was called upon to illustrate a number of aspects of the economics of waste disposal into water courses. Such a firm would tend to minimize the over-all costs associated with disposal of the amount of wastes generated at its optimum level and distribution of output, if all costs of water quality deterioration were either internal or adequately indicated by market valuation.[1] The firm would equate the marginal costs of all relevant alternatives (water quality control measures and residual damages imposed by pollution), and the full marginal costs of each productive process would be considered in making output decisions. The result of such a procedure would be "efficient" in the sense that the firm would produce the largest possible value from the resources it is using. A reasonable objective of public water policy—and one probably commanding widespread agreement—is to work toward maximization of the net value, or net benefits, obtainable from development of the available water supply. Correspondingly, minimizing the costs associated with disposal of the wastes generated by the industry and population of some meaningful water resources planning area (say, a basin) suggests itself as a general goal for public water pollution policy. As such, this objective is too broad to have much meaning, but it is a convenient point of departure.

---

[1] Effects outside the basin were excluded by the assumption that the basin terminates in the ocean. It was also assumed that the firm either produced for competitive markets or had marginal cost pricing imposed upon it.

29

THE ROLE OF PUBLIC POLICY

In contrast to the hypothetical basin of the previous chapter, actual river basins or other water resources areas are inhabited and used by numerous fiscally independent political and economic units. Consequently this is the situation to which public policy must address itself. Actual basins usually have a number of separately managed water-supply intakes, waste discharge points, and public and private intervening stretches of stream or shoreline. In some instances there are navigation facilities, and flow regulation devices as well. A reasonable point of departure for public policy, therefore, is to recognize the technical interdependence between different economic units and between all aspects of water-resource development, and to endeavor to avoid or mitigate the distortions which operation of unregulated markets would produce. This could be accomplished through various combinations of central planning, construction, and operating facilities (dams, sewage treatment facilities, holding lagoons, water-supply treatment facilities, etc.) on the one hand, and a system of charges, bounties, and regulations on the other. With respect to pollution, the objective of these procedures would be to minimize the over-all costs associated with disposal of wastes generated by activities in the basin (all damages and the value of all foregone opportunities plus all direct costs such as treatment, flow regulation, etc.). This would require that public policy endeavor to produce a result similar to that of the basin-wide firm, i.e., that it strive to devise plans and policies which will lead to equalization in all directions of the marginal costs associated with waste disposal. The combination of facilities and their operating procedures, which minimize costs for some initial level of waste generation, would not imply an optimal *distribution* of costs. Therefore, such a system would probably have to be accompanied by a system of taxes and bounties.

In planning a basin-wide waste-disposal system, domestic wastes can probably be taken as a rather straightforward function of population. In some instances, it may also be reasonable to regard industrial wastes as being of quantities and types given independently of the waste disposal and water-supply system and the distribution of costs associated with waste disposal. In these cases the system that minimizes costs can be designed without reference to induced changes in waste generation. However, industrial wastes may vary substantially in quantity and kind owing to changes induced by the cost to the firm of putting wastes into water. The basin-wide firm used earlier for illustrative purposes would generate the "right" amount of wastes and produce the "right" amount and distribution of output, because the costs associated with waste disposal were assumed to be internal to it. The firm, in rationally attempting to maximize profits, would adjust product, process, and output until the marginal net costs of these measures equalled each other, treatment costs, other abatement measures, and the residual damages avoided for the entire system. In an actual basin, industrial plants would not have a similar incentive because the costs associated with waste disposal are predominantly external; a desirable balance between measures affecting wastes delivered to water courses would have to be stimulated by public policy. Ideally, all the costs associated with an increment of waste delivery to the optimum (cost minimizing) basin-wide waste-disposal system would be levied upon the polluting firm and a bounty paid to firms experiencing damages or increased costs. The polluting firm, in turn, would adjust processes and production so as to minimize those costs. In practice, this result could only be approximated by variable effluent charges, variable effluent standards, or other direct controls on the part of the planning agency. The planning of cost-minimizing systems would have to anticipate the effect of such measures on waste generation by polluters.

In order to minimize costs, public policy should consider all feasible alternative water uses (including waste dilution), the effects on quality of the various uses, the losses imposed on other uses by quality deterioration, and the value of all the relevant water derivative uses. Ideally, all relevant alternative system designs and operating procedures would have to be surveyed and a solution derived which would simultaneously indicate the optimum combination of system elements and their operating procedure. If this were successfully done and market prices of basin inputs and outputs adequately reflected social values, the solution would be "efficient." In other words, maximum benefit could be obtained from the available water resources, and, as the latter implies, the costs associated with waste disposal would be minimized.

That this would be a very difficult problem to set up and solve in an ideal fashion for an actual basin, and that doing so would require rather appalling amounts of data, hardly needs to be said. At the present time, data and scientific understanding fall far short of permitting a full and satisfactory solution to the problem. However, stating the problem in this idealized way helps to articulate the implications of economic reasoning for social policy in the pollution field, and to identify areas where improved information can add to more satisfactory pollution control planning. Furthermore, as explained in Chapter VII, recent application of computer technology and mathematical techniques holds promise of providing computational procedures which can approximate optimum solutions for problems of this degree of complexity. The usefulness of these techniques will depend upon the provision of sufficiently detailed and accurate information.

"NON-MARKET" SOCIAL GOALS— CONSTRAINTS ON THE OBJECTIVE

The objectives so far suggested as appropriate for public policy would merely reproduce the results achieved by a firm so situated and integrated as to "internalize" the pollution-caused "externalities." If there were no problems in the manner in which the market registers water quality values, this solution would be quite consistent with the general rationale of a market system.

However, public bodies can and should take account of those aspects of water quality for which market evaluations do not exist, cannot be imputed, or cannot be accepted. These are matters such as general environmental effects, public health, and perhaps others.

Methods of Approach

Two ways of handling the social aspects come to mind. They could be labeled "intangible" and disregarded in the process of planning and designing cost-minimizing waste-disposal systems. Then, when the system designs are actually to be considered for acceptance or rejection by representatives of the public, side information could be provided to aid the decision makers in deciding to accept or reject specific combinations of facilities. This would include information on aesthetic effects, public health, and other matters considered relevant to arriving at a decision in the public interest.

An alternative approach is to include an explicit judgment concerning non-market goals in the process of system design. This can be done by initially treating these goals, expressed in physical terms, as limits or constraints upon the cost minimization objective. For example, if social choice dictated that, in order to maintain environmental amenities,[2] streams must at all times remain aerobic, public policy would be to produce a system which minimizes the real costs associated with waste disposal subject to the constraint that anaerobic conditions are nowhere to develop. Conceivably this would require a very different combination of units with different operating procedures than a system designed without the constraints. Presuming the constraints are effective, i.e., not automatically met if costs are minimized, they would result in a higher cost system than could otherwise have been achieved. The extra cost represents the limitation which the constraint places upon the objective.[3]

Flexibility of the Procedure

Actually constraints upon the objective function need not be limited to those instances where deficiencies in market processes require them.

[2] The general environment is as previously indicated a "public" good. It is possible for persons to express their individual preferences with respect to it by moving. However, this may be socially a very costly way to deal with environmental deterioration.

It may be useful to point out that flood control and the avoidance of pollution damages by flow augmentation or upstream pollution abatement are public goods too, in the sense that providing them for one user provides them for all potential users in the relevant area. On the other hand, they differ from general environmental effects in that it is possible to impute a value to them since they result in the avoidance of tangible costs. The maximum amount which individuals would be willing to pay to avoid damages can be deduced. With respect to environmental effects, there is no such intermediary tangible damage to marketable goods and services.

[3] The distinction between objectives and constraints can be somewhat troublesome when politically determined constraints are involved. "Technological" constraints, which set the physical framework within which maximization (or minimization) is carried out, are usually fairly clear-cut. In a pollution problem such a constraint might be that water cannot flow uphill. Public policy constraints, however, can be viewed as requirements set on certain results which constrain the effort devoted to the attainment of others (objectives). In a pollution problem one of the policy constraints might be the one outlined in the text.

As a generalization, the following distinction has been proposed. "A practicable distinction between constraints and objectives might go as follows: A requirement is a constraint if (a) it must not be violated at any cost however high or with any probability however low, and (b) if there is no gain or advantage in overfulfilling it. On the other hand, a requirement is one of the objectives of the firm if it can be violated, though at a cost or penalty, or if there is an advantage in overfulfilling it." Robert Dorfman, "Operations Research," *American Economic Review*, Sept. 1960, pp. 614-15. Obviously, politically determined constraints often do not fully meet the rigorous conditions described and certainly those set out in a model intended to deal with pollution would have difficulty in doing so. Hence the great importance of not considering constraints immutable and of testing the sensitivity of costs to them.

The decision model framework itself is flexible enough to incorporate any constraints public policy wishes to impose upon the achievement of efficiency with respect to measurable pollution costs. Indeed, the objective need not be based upon efficiency at all. For example, the goal of "cleaning up the streams," if its requirements can be made explicit, could be posed to the exclusion of all others, or it could be constrained in various ways. Achieving it would still involve a problem of some interest and significance, since a number of alternative methods could be incorporated into the system design and therefore the problem of "optimum" system design still exists.

It must be said, however, that while this type of framework is very flexible and can be used to combine efficiency and policy goals, the inclusion of the latter means that the procedure need not, and probably will not, lead to a full optimum but only to a sub-optimum, i..e, an optimum subject to higher-level decisions constraining the minimization (maximization) process.[4] From the point of view of achieving maximum welfare, this indicates that the policy constraints should be considered "provisional" and viewed as a subject matter for research and study in order to expand their meaning with respect to the preferences of society. One way of studying them from this point of view is to test their cost sensitivity. By varying a constraint by small amounts, redetermining the optimum system, and collating the change in costs with the associated physical changes (i.e., effects on oxygen levels, appearance, aquatic life, etc., in specific stretches of stream), information can be provided which permits considered choices to be made by representatives of the public. This provides a means of exploring a collective demand function identified through political procedures, thus permitting a closer approach to the goal of meeting the preferences of society.

One useful way of stating the results of variation of constraints which represent goals not directly incorporable in the objective function (i.e., which are not valued directly by, or imputable from, the market) is in terms of what they must "at least be worth." For example, if a judgment were made that algae growth is to be restricted (say, because of its effect on the appearance of water) beyond the point indicated by the

[4] For an interesting and instructive discussion of optima and suboptima, see Charles J. Hitch and Roland N. McKean, *The Economics of Defense in the Nuclear Age* (Cambridge: Harvard University Press, 1960), Part II, or for discussion more directly addressing water resources issues, Roland N. McKean, *Efficiency in Government Through Systems Analysis* (New York: John Wiley & Sons, 1958).

cost-minimizing solution, it would not be possible to say precisely what the avoided destruction of aesthetic pleasure is worth. However, by comparing the optimum system with and without the constraint, it is possible to indicate what the *least* value is that must be attached to the increment of pleasure in order to make that level of control procedures worth while.

The design of efficient systems and experimentation with the constraints require large amounts of data and extensive knowledge of physical and economic relationships. The work can be greatly facilitated by rapid and flexible techniques for computing both the physical characteristics of pollution and the actual minimization (maximization) procedure.

STREAM SPECIALIZATION TECHNIQUES— CLASSIFICATION AND ZONING

It has been aptly written that "It can in fact be argued that the *chief* gain from systematic analysis is the stimulus that it provides for the invention of better systems."[5] One possibility that suggests itself in this regard is the incorporation of specialized streams or sections of streams into the water resources system design. For example, if the maintenance of fish habitat for sport fishing is a valuable undertaking in a particular sub-basin, stream specialization may permit a lower real cost of waste disposal (including of course foregone recreational opportunities) than would be the case if conditions suitable for sport fish culture were maintained throughout the basin.

Advantages of Specialization

Under some circumstances it may be efficient to designate that certain streams or stretches of streams are to be used primarily for, say, recreation and others primarily for the disposal of wastes. This can be done only by strictly enforced stream standards or by explicit zoning. The advantages appear to be reinforced by several technical-economic factors. For example, the rate at which water absorbs oxygen from the atmosphere is directly proportional to the oxygen deficit (i.e., the amount by which dissolved oxygen falls short of saturation). Hence the lower the dissolved oxygen falls, the greater is the rate at which atmos-

[5] Hitch and McKean, *op. cit.,* p. 187. Emphasis in the original.

pheric reaeration occurs. Accordingly, a body of water in which dissolved oxygen is almost depleted is a very efficient assimilator of oxygen-demanding wastes while still maintaining aerobic conditions. In addition, the ability of a stream to purify itself of putrescible and infectious materials means that it is often less costly to treat industrial intake water, the major part of which is for cooling, than to provide extensive treatment of wastes. Also in a stream used predominantly for waste disposal and where loadings have gone sufficiently high to require extensive treatment, the presence of plant nutrients in effluents might play a somewhat different role than in waters devoted primarily to recreation and public water supplies. In the latter, taste, odor, and treatment problems presented by algae might well make expensive tertiary treatment of wastes, or land disposal techniques desirable. In the former, however, the presence of nitrates might be beneficial. Should the oxygen content become exhausted as a result of heavy organic pollution, nitrates provide a reserve of oxygen which can be utilized by bacteria thus preventing septic conditions and attendant odor nuisances. Indeed, during the summer months sodium nitrate is sometimes added to streams to avoid the generation of offensive odors.[6] Care must be taken to protect downstream values by specifying zones primarily intended for the disposal of wastes.

Similarly, specialized recreation waters might present notable advantages. A zoned area that is kept free of industrial and municipal development would yield visual advantages as well as improved water quality. Dissolved oxygen could be kept high without encountering the plant nutrient problems that extensive orthodox treatment of wastes cannot avoid.

Methods of Analysis

If all relevant values could be measured by a monetary standard, a variety of situations utilizing differing standards for different streams or stretches of stream might be explored in order to approach an optimum system. In following this procedure, cognizance would have to be given to special advantages of location for certain industries. For example, in computing the costs of maintaining a stream for recreational purposes the higher treatment costs of industries located there

---

[6] For a defense of nitrates in effluents delivered into streams heavily loaded with municipal and industrial wastes, see Louis Klein, *Aspects of River Pollution* (New York: Academic Press, Inc., 1957), chapter 14.

and the higher costs or less desirable location of prospective industries must be included. This is the type of case in which it would be extremely easy to neglect "spillovers" or external diseconomies. Such diseconomies may take the form not only of fairly immediate, albeit indirect, costs but also of inflexibilities in future stream use introduced by a classification or zoning made at a particular time. It should be noted, however, that in an analysis of the type outlined, the classification would tend to grow out of the procedure followed, not be imposed upon it.

If recreation (or any public goal) cannot be valued explicitly, but its physical requirements must be treated as constraints, an analogous type of analysis may still be useful. Various stream specialization possibilities may be explored and the decision as to whether the public interest is adequately protected left to representatives of the public. If scheme I, for example, has a measurable real cost $1 million less than scheme II (utilizing stream specialization), society may choose scheme I even though some unknown (but implicitly less than $1 million) value of recreation opportunities are foregone. Good decisions would be dependent upon accurate description of relevant but incommensurable variables such as the physical effects of the plans and their impact upon (say) the use of recreation facilities.

On a more specific level as well, cost analysis of zoning would be useful. By experimentally spacing industrial and municipal development in various ways and following a cost minimization analysis, valuable, but not conclusive, information may be obtained. A careful spacing of industrial developments may, for example, significantly reduce treatment costs. This information would have to be weighed against other factors, perhaps not initially included in the analysis, i.e. various kinds of locational disadvantages, possible increases in commuting costs, etc. Thus while such analysis would not necessarily provide a ready-made solution, it would furnish important and socially relevant information which is not presently considered or even available when industrial locations are planned.

A GENERAL PROBLEM IN EVALUATION— THE DESIGN FLOW

A matter of general significance for the evaluation of pollution abatement policies is the choice of critical streamflow for which protection is to be sought. This problem occurs because the concentration of most pollutants in streams is inversely related to the rate of streamflow. An analogous consideration arises in regard to criteria for the design of flood-control structures, except that the focus is upon high rather than low flows.

Protection against pollution damages during the lowest imaginable flow would be roughly analogous to protection against the "maximum probable flood."[7] In present practice, designing pollution abatement facilities so as to achieve the maximum degree of protection is generally considered infeasible and some lesser goal is chosen—usually a conventional rule-of-thumb flow standard. The choice of design flows is central to the alternative cost calculation of low-flow augmentation benefits as presently conducted and to pollution planning generally.

In practice, design flows for pollution abatement purposes consist of two elements—the period over which a flow is averaged and the interval between low flows. In the following discussion these will be respectively referred to as the "period" and the "interval." Thus a treatment plant may be designed to prevent dissolved oxygen from falling below 4 ppm during a mean seven-day low flow with a once in seven years probability of recurrence. Obviously, this will be a different plant from one designed for a mean seven-day low flow expected to recur every ten years. Indeed, in terms of cfs discharge, averaging over fifteen rather than seven days can make more difference than shifting from a once-in-twenty-year to a once-in-ten-year interval.[8]

---

[7] Luna B. Leopold and Thomas Maddock, Jr., *The Flood Control Controversy* (New York: The Ronald Press, 1954), p. 117. Some descriptive material on design-flow problems with respect to low-flow augmentation is found in C. H. J. Hull and H. Clark Carbaugh, *Report No. VI of the Low-Flow Augmentation Project* (Baltimore: The Johns Hopkins University, August 1959 and January 1961), p. 20. The latter study points out that while the setting of waste-treatment requirements is the prerogative of the states, the criteria used for determining the design waste capacity of streams vary from state to state, and that in fact many states have no specific design criteria. The benefit-cost ratio of low-flow augmentation projects can—as presently calculated—be appreciably altered by differences in design flow.

The analogy with the design of flood-control reservoirs is not complete since in the case of floods the possible catastrophe resulting from a failure of the dam itself is a significant consideration. Blair Bower pointed this out to the author in private correspondence.

[8] For examples, see the conveniently arranged charts entitled "Drought Duration vs. Severity" in Clarence J. Velz and John J. Gannon, *Drought Flow of Michigan Streams* (Lansing: Department of Environmental Health, School of Public Health, University of Michigan, in co-operation with Michigan Water Resources Commission, 1960).

From the point of view of basin-wide water resources planning, both the period and the interval are significant because they can both affect the optimum combination of abatement measures and their optimum scale.

If the probable damages of pollution could be completely integrated into a monetary measure of value, the difficulties presented by the choice of period and interval for design-flow purposes would in principle be amenable to fairly straightforward marginal analysis. In essence, the procedure would be to extend protection in such a way that the costs of all relevant means of avoiding damages of waste disposal and the mathematical expectation of damages avoided were equalized at the margin, taking into consideration both the period and the interval. The optimal combination of the two would depend upon the character of the relationship between duration of low flow and damages.

In present practice the design flow for treatment plants and flow-augmentation projects is ordinarily chosen arbitrarily (indeed, often specified by state law) with a favorite apparently being the seven-day once-in-ten-year flow. It is sometimes suggested that the averaging period should correspond to the elapsed time between the delivery of waste to the stream and the critical point on the oxygen sag. While this period may have some relevance because of the relationship between stream velocity (incorporated in the sag formula) and quantity of flow, the choice cannot reasonably be made on this basis alone, since it also involves a decision as to the appropriate stringency of stream standards. In addition, the D.O. standard is, of course, only one possible criterion. Unfortunately the difficulties of damage estimation and problems involved in the treatment of politically determined constraints do not permit a completely satisfactory alternative to be offered.

Insofar as market type damages (including imposed treatment costs) are concerned, cost minimization, in principle, can proceed within the constraints as previously outlined. It is in the specification of design flow for the constraints that serious conceptual difficulties occur. Since the goals represented by politically determined constraints cannot be directly evaluated, the flows to which the constraints are to apply must in some manner be determined by the judgment of public officials. Types of information could, however, be developed which would contribute to intelligent judgment. If a dissolved oxygen standard were among the constraints (say, based on recreation considerations), it would be important to know how fish kills are related to the persistence of low-flow conditions. Is any averaging justified, or are fish killed if the D.O. falls below a given level even briefly? In regard to public health standards (in those instances where stream standards are relevant) it would, for example, be essential to have information about the relationships between the chronic and acute effects of certain toxicants found in water supplies.

Furthermore, cost sensitivity analysis in the manner suggested earlier could contribute valuable information for the social decision-making process. Essentially, the costs (in terms of the objective) of the constraints would be analyzed in two ways. Different levels of each constraint and varying design flows would be related to corresponding (sub) optimum waste-disposal systems. The cost, if not the feasibility, of such analysis depends upon efficient means for forecasting the physical characteristics of receiving waters, over large areas, at various flows and with various disposal systems, as well as improved techniques for determining (constrained) optimum systems.

CONCLUDING COMMENTS

Within the general framework of a market system, there are rather clear-cut reasons to suppose that public intervention can improve performance with respect to disposal of wastes into water bodies. Not only can government intervention improve efficiency as measured in terms of market values but it can and should take explicit cognizance of extra-market values. Since the character of water courses in heavily populated areas is such that interdependency between uses is inevitable, a major problem confronting public policy is to gauge accurately the significance of various interdependencies and foster the efficient multipurpose use of the water resource.

It has been noted that system planning would ideally consider all alternative water uses (including pollution abatement), effects on quality of the various uses, losses imposed on other uses by quality deterioration, and the value of water derivative uses. All feasible alternative system designs and operating procedures would be considered and a solution derived which simultaneously indicated the optimum combination of system elements and operating procedures, in light of the objective and constraints of the system. Unfortunately the inherent complexity of the problem, plus conceptual and informational deficiencies, make *fully* optimum solutions an unattainable goal.[9] Nevertheless, an approach utilizing models of the general type outlined in this chapter, preferably programmed for machine solution, could provide significantly improved information to aid the social decision-making process.

In addition to any direct merit which such an approach may have for public policy, setting out basin-wide pollution control problems in comparatively formal terms has useful side effects. For one thing, it requires an explicit and unambiguous statement of objectives. Moreover, the need to identify relevant relations and specify them rigorously can play an important part in revealing inadequacies in information. Consequently, potentially fruitful avenues of research are revealed.

Planning for pollution control, of course, cannot await ideal tools and data. Consequently, it is important to note that viewing pollution in terms of interdependencies and as a problem in system planning, can have beneficial results even though fully ideal techniques cannot be immediately applied. This means emphasis upon competitive and complementary relationships with other aspects of water resources development, upon the relative cost (including all opportunity costs) of alternatives, upon the possible cost reduction achievable by marginal tradeoffs, and upon the analysis of costs where incommensurable objectives are relevant. In any case—whether systematic, sophisticated, optimizing methods[10] or more rough and ready procedures are used—improved information of an economic, physical, and biological character is necessary for comprehensive planning which strives to attain economic goals. It may be noted that the traditional focus of pollution policy and research has been much more upon the problems presented by specific pollution sources than upon planning integrated systems for areas linked by pollution-induced physical and economic interdependencies.

The primary objective of Part I has been to outline a conceptual foundation for public policy which helps identify areas where research should be able to improve the planning process. Broadly, four such areas now suggest themselves:

[9] Arbitrariness in the specification of constraints, the absence of fully satisfactory means of introducing risk preferences, and the inevitable uncertainty involved in forecasting and planning for future changes in economic and technological variables militate against achievement of fully optimum decisions. In addition, it is impossible to avoid uncertainties arising out of the use of market relationships as representations of value. This implies that flexibility and adaptability must be considered as valuable attributes in plans for waste-disposal systems.

[10] See Chapter VII.

1. Physical and biological research aimed at more accurate and flexible prediction of the physical characteristics of polluted waters at specific points and under widely varying conditions.

2. Physical, biological, and economic research aimed at determining the likely range and relative costs of alternatives for controlling water quality in an optimal manner.

3. Research aimed at extending knowledge of the costs of damages and foregone opportunities imposed by pollutants in various concentrations and under varying conditions. This includes physical, biological, and social science research on the effects of pollution.[11]

4. Research aimed at providing improved means of simultaneously and rapidly dealing with numerous constraints and interrelated variables in the solution of models.

These areas inevitably overlap to some degree, but in Part II they are taken up roughly in the order indicated.

APPENDICES TO CHAPTER IV

I—Benefit-Cost Analysis and the "Constrained Cost Minimization" Framework

For those who are familiar with "benefit-cost" analysis, it may be useful to restate the "constrained cost minimization" framework, outlined in this chapter, in terms of benefits and costs. Those results of a planned system of waste disposal which can be thought of as reduced damages adequately

---

[11] "Basic" research directed toward improved fundamental understanding of the physical, chemical, and biological aspects of water as found in nature and as altered by man is clearly relevant to points 1, 2 and 3. Such research may be expected to widen the scope of feasible alternatives and improve understanding and prediction of their effects. The focus of the present study is, however, upon defining the types of research, in economics and the natural sciences, whose significance for improved planning and operation of waste-disposal systems is rather clearly in view and generally does not depend upon additions to "basic" scientific knowledge. The latter, while more significant in the long run, can not satisfactorily be planned on the basis of the requirements of efficient system planning and operation. Numerous references to problem areas where improved basic understanding could make a large contribution are made at later points but there is no attempt to outline a comprehensive and specific program of *basic* research.

valued by market-based calculations, may be treated as benefits with which the costs (construction and operation of structures) can be compared. If all pollution effects can be adequately valued, the benefit-cost relationship has its conventional meaning and minimization of the costs associated with waste disposal is formally identical with maximization of the (positive) difference between benefits and costs. If constraints are admitted, they must be viewed as objectives or requirements which must be attained but which are not necessarily associated with any benefit to be valued in terms of money. The objective of cost minimization may then be alternatively stated as being the maximization of the positive difference between benefits and costs or the minimization of the negative difference, whichever the appropriate case may be, provided that the requirements of the constraints are met. It may be that a particular system cannot be carried beyond the constraints without decreasing net benefits or, what is the same thing, increasing the total costs associated with waste disposal (costs of the project plus damages and foregone opportunities). If total costs continue to decline (equivalently if net benefits continue to increase or net costs continue to decline), this means that the marginal product of investment in abatement is positive. Since calculable pollution damage takes a number of forms some of which may be associated with the characteristics to which constraints are applied and some not, it would be quite possible for the over-all benefits (as defined above) to be exceeded by the over-all costs of an abatement system even though the marginal relationship is the reverse. In this case the negative over-all ratio cannot, of course, be taken to indicate an inefficient or undesirable project. The relevant questions are: (1) are the constraints met, and (2) does it pay to contrive to invest in abatement after the constraints are met, i.e. is the marginal efficiency of investment positive? In other words, once constraints are set by social policy, the best system may be viewed as one that meets them at minimum cost and continues to expand (abstracting from possible budget constraints) as long as total costs associated with waste disposal fall. In those instances where a constraint is applied to a (stream or water supply) quality characteristic (say, for public health reasons), the improvement of which can profitably be carried beyond the point required, because it (say) reduces corrosion damage, the constraint will not be effective in an optimum abatement system.

In practice, formal benefit-cost analyses of water-quality improvement have been limited to the evaluation of low-flow augmentation with water supply and sewage treatment usually the only alternatives considered. In federal agency evaluations, industrial and navigation benefits have been calculated in terms of avoided costs, and benefits to public water supplies have been similarly obtained. However, the latter category of benefits differs from those attributable to industrial treatment costs (and those which could, under the appropriate circumstances, be attributed to agriculture and conceivably to recreation), in that they are, to a large degree, not a representation or an imputation of market-type valuation. They differ also from benefits determined for power and navigation in multipurpose projects, where alternative costs are usually used as measures of benefit, in that the

latter evaluations presuppose an existing or developable market demand
that can be met more cheaply by the use of public capital.

To the extent that public supplies are treated for hardness, corrosiveness,
and potability, and such treatment costs are avoided, market-type benefits
can accrue, although decisions on these types of treatment are likely themselves to have been made without much analysis of costs and benefits. On
the other hand, public health considerations—which are inevitably a factor
in the treatment of public supplies—are in a different category. In their
case, alternative treatment costs are really a sort of stand-in for drinking
water standards which are not based upon market valuations.

A similar point may be made in regard to pollution abatement benefits,
which are figured as the reduced cost of sewage treatment beyond the primary level, and which have bulked large in a number of evaluations.
These benefits are also not based in any direct fashion upon market valuations but really relate to the achievement of certain receiving water standards. These standards may be derived from recreational, aesthetic, or public health considerations. More often they do not arise from explicit
analysis of particular situations but are based on conventional standards
and design flows. The formulation in the text does not avoid such ex-
ternally imposed standards, but it does distinguish them from market-type
benefits, while the federal agency practice does not. The latter arbitrarily
transposes a politically determined requirement into a "benefit."

II—Property Values

It is sometimes suggested that changes in property values in the vicinity
of a stream can be used as a proxy for the value of the desirable effects
achievable by pollution-abatement policies, thus avoiding explicit consideration of a number of the complexities considered in this chapter. Aside from
the great practical difficulties involved in distinguishing the effects of pollution control or abatement from the multitude of others involved in the
determination of property values over time, and the fact that property
values do not yield information directly relevant to efficient system design,
this approach appears to have other serious shortcomings.

It is possible to imagine conditions under which property values might
reflect the primary benefits of a water resources project quite closely. This
could occur where one factor is completely fixed in supply and where other
factors are entirely mobile. The rise in price of the fixed factor would
then be a measure of the discounted value of the net return of the project,
if markets functioned in an unobstructed fashion. Thus, the rise in value of
land brought under irrigation is a measure of the discounted net return to
an irrigation project. However, a rise in the value of residential and commercial land in the area would represent primarily, if not entirely, a transfer
having its counterpart in a reduction of values in the areas from which
labor resources are drawn.

In the case of enhancement of values due to pollution abatement, the situation is much more complex. From the point of view of national benefits (real costs avoided) a rise in the value of proximate properties simultaneously measures too much and too little. To some degree the increase in value may result from a discounting of the net advantage of locating in the area serviced by the newly cleansed stream. Costs of production may initially be lower than in other locations and part of the consequent rise in values is indicative of a net advantage, other things remaining equal. In addition, residential property prices may rise more than they otherwise would because of the recreational amenities of the area. If this part of the over-all increase could be segregated, it would be a partial proxy for the increase in welfare provided by improved recreation opportunity. However, the relevant share of the total rise is inextricably intermingled with the portions that represent a mere transfer and that are counterbalanced by decrements elsewhere. Moreover, the increased welfare enjoyed by many of those using the new recreation opportunity is not necessarily registered in property values at all so long as public access to those opportunities prevails. The new opportunity may be reflected in larger expenditures for gasoline, for example, rather than for land. Similar considerations hold for aesthetic and general environmental conditions. It appears that changes in property values are an inadequate and possibly highly deceptive representation of the real gains from pollution control. Only in the case of industrial uses does it seem that a fairly satisfactory approach can be worked out. Even here, more direct attempts at estimation are probably in order because of the problem involved in isolating the specific effects of pollution abatement and the probable lack of transferability of the results.

Part II

RESEARCH NEEDS

V

The Effect of Wastes on Receiving
Water – Some Computational
and Scientific Problems

THE NEED FOR AN EFFICIENT AND FLEXIBLE MEANS
OF CALCULATION AND SOME PROBLEMS
INVOLVED IN DEVISING IT

Any waste-disposal planning procedure *that takes into account extensive reaches of receiving water and a variety of water-quality control
measures* requires an efficient means of determining the concentration
of pollutants at specific points, as a function of certain conditioning
factors. These factors include quantities and characteristics of wastes
delivered at specific outfalls, condition of stream flow, water temperature, and other relevant variables. Without an underlying technique of
this character, the economic and other effects of alternative system
designs cannot be adequately predicted and system planning for waste
disposal cannot be satisfactorily done.

Problems Involved

Providing the required technique presents two basic problems. The
first is the conceptual and mathematical problem of devising a model
which comprehends the relevant relationships and is amenable to rapid
calculation. The other is empirical specification of parameters for the
functional relationships in the model, that is to say, the specific numeri-
cal effect of a change in one variable (or set of variables) on the others.

The former problem is presently being explored by the Taft Sanitary
Engineering Center. The objective is to provide an electronic computer
program that will permit rapid and flexible tracing of the effects of a
change at upstream points throughout the downstream areas included
in the analysis. Parameters for the initial model will be obtained from
accepted empirical results, traditional rules of thumb, or, where neces-

sary, they will be assumed. In essence the model will keep track of all accretions and reductions of pollutants along the stream. Keeping track of conservative pollutants is relatively much less difficult since dilution is substantially the only factor that affects their concentration.

Degradable Pollutants

Degradable pollutants, which do not remain constant in quantity or form and whose effects on the stream are conditioned by a number of variables, are not necessarily the most destructive pollutants, but they present the greatest difficulties for establishing appropriate empirical relations. Actually the degradable organics have been the subject of by far the largest share of research in sanitary engineering and related fields. Nevertheless, there appear to be comparatively serious gaps in knowledge that inhibit the precise application of a model of the type previously sketched. For one thing, several factors that were formerly of comparatively minor importance may be coming to bear upon the oxygen balance of water bodies. For example, synthetic detergents, cooling water discharge, and other pollutants are capable of affecting the rate of BOD and/or reoxygenation ability.

Moreover, the traditional focus of research has been upon point sources of pollution and effects directly traceable to them, rather than upon an entire area (say, a basin) tied together by physical interdependencies. The difficulties of analysis increase rapidly as the area taken into consideration expands. An illustration of the difference in orientation required for basin-wide planning is provided by the oxygen "sag." As was described in Chapter II, biochemical oxygen demand is exerted in two stages. If untreated waste is expelled into a water course, the first stage BOD tends to result in a distinct sag of dissolved oxygen in the receiving water. It is upon the low point of this sag that treatment plant design ordinarily hinges. After substantial recovery from the primary oxygen sag, a second stage BOD commences in which BOD is once more high and tends to deplete D.O. but results in a less distinct and less deep sag. In most instances the second stage BOD is essentially a continuation of the first; however, in some instances stream water may appear to be completely purified between the two stages. The second zone appears five to seven days downstream.[1] The second stage is ordi-

---

[1] See Edmond Leclerc, "The Self-Purification of Streams and the Relationship Between Chemical and Biological Tests," in *Waste Treatment*, ed., Peter C. G. Isaac (New York, Oxford, London, Paris: Pergamon Press, 1960), p. 286.

narily neglected in the design of individual treatment plants, where the focus is upon limited stretches of stream and, accordingly, it has received comparatively much less attention. However, it may be of substantial importance in planning an optimum waste disposal system for an entire basin because of its influence on assimilative capacity at remote points. Other instances of differences in the character of problems encountered in basin-wide and "point" planning are noted in the following discussion.

DEGRADABLE POLLUTANTS, ALGAE, AND OXYGEN BALANCE

Since degradable organic wastes are gradually "assimilated" in the receiving waters, a model used to predict the condition of such waters at specific points of use must incorporate a method of accurately following the course of the process and registering significant effects which it may produce. Two interrelated elements are particularly significant in the process. One is the breakdown of the organic waste products by the stream biota, because it draws directly upon the water's dissolved oxygen. The other is the conversion of organic waste into plant nutrients because of the stimulation that it may provide to aquatic plant growth —most importantly algae. The two elements are related, since the algae growths induced by the residual products of biological degradation are both creators and utilizers of dissolved oxygen. The following discussion focuses upon the prediction of algae growth and its effect upon the oxygen balance because it is in these areas that some of the most difficult, unresolved, problems appear to lie.

Algae Growth

The problems presented by excessive algae growth have recently elicited much discussion because, with the expansion of population and economic activity, the amount of plant nutrient entering water courses has increased rapidly in recent years. In the absence of rather fundamental changes in sewage treatment, this tendency can be expected to continue.

Moreover, by no means all plant nutrients enter water courses from sewage outfalls. A substantial but not precisely known quantity results from agricultural and urban use of fertilizers and various other land

sources. Analysis of the relations between load changes at sewage outfalls and stream conditions would, of course, require a fairly precise
separation between waste water and other sources of plant nutrients.
This problem has received only very limited attention.

The principal plant nutrient products of organic waste degradation
are nitrogen and phosphorus. Discussion of the algae problem has in
the past focused upon these.

Attention has centered on "available" (ammonia and nitrates) nitrogen rather than upon the total nitrogen content of the waste water. One
recent study proceeding on a regional basis has focused upon "available"
nitrogen as the significant type for the prediction of algae growth.[2]
However, it might be argued that for long, heavily loaded, stretches of
stream, the total nitrogen content of the effluent is more significant since
bacterial action in the receiving water causes the process of "nitrification" to continue. It may be, of course, that both total nitrogen and
"available" nitrogen are important since the latter may give rise to algae
"blooms" in the receiving water while the former adds to the inventory
of nitrogen. The total "available" nitrogen question is of considerable
significance since it bears importantly on both the calculation of the
receiving waters' assimilative capacity and upon the choice of appropriate treatment technique. If total nitrogen is the critical variable, conventional treatment can be carried to as high a level as possible to the
benefit of the stream, since total nitrogen falls continuously, if gradually,
as BOD reduction is advanced. However, the only way to remove most
of the nitrogen from sewage is by means of tertiary treatment, a typical
means of sludge disposal, irrigation, and the like. "Available" nitrogen
tends to increase as sewage treatment advances, but standard treatment
can be operated so as to vary within limits the amount of nitrates relative
to total nitrogen.[3]

[2] Senate Select Committee on National Water Resources, Committee Print 29,
Water Requirements for Pollution Abatement, by George W. Reid, 1960. This
document is a pioneering attempt to forecast waste assimilative capacity on a
regional basis.
[3] The possibilities of treating for plant nutrients are discussed in more detail
in Chapter VI. An additional matter should perhaps be mentioned once more
at this point. When nitrification is permitted to occur in the stream rather than
in the treatment plant, a demand is made upon dissolved oxygen by the nitrifying
bacteria while, on the other hand, a well-nitrified effluent provides a buffer
against the development of septic conditions. A good discussion of this matter is
found in Louis Klein, *Aspects of River Pollution* (New York: Academic Press,
Inc., 1957), p. 555 ff. One researcher has indicated if sewage is discharged into
an estuary with a long period of retention, as much as 30 per cent of the total
BOD may be accounted for by the nitrification stage. See comment by S. H.

To further complicate the picture, a number of specialists believe that phosphorus rather than nitrogen is usually the critical agent in algae growth. Nitrogen apparently is comparatively more abundant in most water bodies receiving wastes, and at least part of the nitrogen requirement can be obtained from the atmosphere via the air-water interface.[4]

Photosynthetic Oxygen

Another major factor determining the capacity of receiving waters to assimilate degradable organic wastes, is the rate at which the water absorbs oxygen. Ordinarily this is characterized as an empirical constant (k_2), the magnitude of which is a function of factors determining absorption of atmospheric oxygen through the air-water interface.[5] However, at least periodically, oxygen is generated photosynthetically in streams supporting aquatic plant growth. The significance of photosynthesis in the determination of the oxygen balance of waters is a matter of some disagreement and is of course related to the plant nutrient question.

Photosynthetic oxygen production is affected by factors such as cloudiness, time of day, turbidity, and temperature. During the night, algae extract oxygen from the water, thus producing a regular diurnal cycle of dissolved oxygen. But, during periods of bright sunlight and during warm seasons of the year tremendous amounts of oxygen are generated photosynthetically in streams, lakes and estuaries. Several times the quantity obtained through exchange across the interface may be produced in this way. A large share may be dissipated into the atmosphere as the oxygen absorptive capacity of water is limited. In water heavily loaded with oxygen-demanding wastes, however, photosynthetically produced oxygen can add to D.O. Nevertheless, sanitary engineering opinion and practice typically neglect this source of oxygen, except insofar as it implicitly enters the empirical reaeration coefficient (k_2), which includes whatever influences exist in a body of water at the time the samples are taken. The traditional reasons for attempting

Jenkins on James R. Simpson, "Biochemistry of Anaerobic Digestion," in *Waste Treatment, op. cit.,* p. 46.

[4] Based on a conversation with E. C. Tsivoglou, Field Operations Section, Robert A. Taft Sanitary Engineering Center, U.S. Public Health Service, Cincinnati.

[5] A good explanation may be found in Gordon Maskew Fair and John Charles Geyer, *Water Supply and Waste-Water Disposal* (New York: John Wiley and Sons, 1956), p. 843.

to exclude photosynthetic oxygen from oxygen sag calculations are that it is an undependable source, or that the oxygen produced is subsequently consumed by algae respiration and decay and therefore of no net benefit to the water body. Some engineers, however, are doubtful of the accuracy of calculations of assimilative capacity that do not explicitly include consideration of photosynthetic oxygen, because the supply is large, if variable, and consequently can bias predictions based on empirical relationships unless its effects can be quantified. Furthermore, at least one student of oxygen balance has argued that there is not likely to be a straightforward equivalence between oxygen production and oxygen demand by algae and that in many instances algae can be expected to contribute a net supply.[6] In this regard it may be noted that in stabilization ponds photosynthesis supplies a large proportion of the oxygen that bacteria utilize in degradation of wastes. Similarly in other impounded or comparatively quiescent bodies of water, photosynthetic oxygenation may be of special importance.[7] Moreover, since the heaviest periods of oxygen production by aquatic plants tend to coincide with periods of hot weather and low stream flow, it appears that the close management of heavily-used streams may require explicit attention to the rate of photosynthetic oxygen production.

It should not be underemphasized that algae growth may have highly undesirable effects that have nothing to do with their possible effects on the oxygen balance. They can affect taste, odor, and appearance and create treatment problems. This means that algae growth may pose significant costs, which must be evaluated in conjunction with its effects upon the BOD assimilation potential of the receiving water.

Other Influences on the Oxygen Balance

The oxygen balance in natural waters is an extremely complex phenomenon. While the role of photosynthetic oxygen is a striking case of incomplete knowledge, other aspects of reaeration also are not completely understood. It is proven that various substances in domestic and industrial sewage alter reaeration rates via the interface. For ex-

[6] C. H. J. Hull in discussion of Donald J. O'Connor, "Oxygen Balance of an Estuary," *Journal of the Sanitary Engineering Division, Proceedings of the American Society of Civil Engineers,* Vol. 86, No. SA 6, Nov. 1960, Part I, pp. 105-120.
[7] See comment of P. S. Bakels in discussion of Edmond Leclerc's "The Self-Purification of Streams and the Relationship Between Chemical and Biological Tests" in *Waste Treatment, op. cit.,* p. 315.

ample, under laboratory conditions as little as 1 ppm of anionic synthetic detergent can reduce the reaeration coefficient by 20-30 per cent.[8] Apparently the over-all effect of mixed pollutants found in various types of sewage has not been adequately studied, nor is it well enough understood to permit rather precise predictions of assimilative capacity under differing conditions of pollution.[9]

While attention is usually focused on the factors governing reaeration in discussions of the oxygen sag, the rate at which biochemical oxygen demand is exerted (the other factor in the oxygen sag equation) is equally complex. The rate of BOD is affected by a variety of factors including temperature, remaining oxygen demand, configuration of the stream bed, and toxicity of the receiving waters.

CONCLUSIONS

Accurate knowledge of physical and biological relationships in water bodies is an essential prerequisite to the design and operation of optimum waste-disposal systems. Furthermore, an efficient means of calculating the effects on receiving water of changes in amounts and types of waste loads, streamflow, temperature, and other relevant variables is necessary. The above discussion is merely illustrative of remaining problems in the quest to comprehend and put into a systematic framework the amazingly complex phenomena that occur in water bodies.

Deficiencies in knowledge become particularly evident when water bodies receiving heavy waste loads are considered as interrelated wholes. Increased study of how chemical, physical, and biological phenomena (including algae growth) affect oxygen balance should increase the possibility of accurate prediction.

However, research along unorthodox lines is also to be encouraged. For example, the application of multivariate statistical procedures in this field appears to be in its infancy.[10] Perhaps future research should explore the possibility of a more definitely empirical approach to water

[8] Louis Klein, *Aspects of River Pollution, op. cit.,* p. 141.
[9] M. C. Rand, "Concepts of Surface Reaeration—A Critical Review," *Sewage and Industrial Wastes,* November 1957.
[10] The limited amount of work of this character which has come to the author's attention yielded some interesting results. See M. A. Churchill and R. A. Buckingham, "Statistical Method for Analysis of Stream-Purification Capacity," *Sewage and Industrial Wastes,* April 1956.

phenomena. It may be possible to isolate relationships that can be depended on with considerable confidence even though their chemical, biological, and physical bases are not well understood.[11]

[11] This does not mean that the patterns should not be investigated to discover why they show regularities. But as has been recently written in a somewhat different context, "For certain purposes, of course, none of this matters. If a pattern is reproducible, we can use it both for the control of the social organization and for prediction of the future, just as we can use Boyle's law as a macrophenomenon notwithstanding that in the kinetic theory of gases, the component molecules may differ in speed and direction just as much as individual cricketers or gamblers." M. G. Kendall, "Natural Law and the Social Sciences," *Journal of the Royal Statistical Society,* Vol. 124, Part I, 1961.

VI

Deficiencies in Technical and Economic Knowledge – Damages, Treatment, and Abatement Costs

Regardless of the exact methodology adopted, effective economic analysis of pollution policies requires knowledge of costs. Precise application of the cost minimization model sketched in Part I would require such knowledge in detailed form for extensive ranges of the pertinent variables.

As indicted in Part I, relevant costs include not only direct outlays for treatment plants, flow-augmentation projects, etc., but, equally important, the costs of pollution damages. Discussion of a number of the more significant aspects of the specification of costs and the assignment of tentative water quality constraints, where costs cannot be satisfactorily specified, is undertaken in this chapter. The objective is to identify areas where improved information can contribute to economically rational and socially meaningful waste-disposal policy. Unfortunately any breakdown of these matters into separate topics inevitably produces some overlaps or neglects some interdependencies.

DAMAGES, TREATMENT, AND ALTERNATIVE WATER QUALITY CONTROL MEASURES

This section deals with damages to industry, municipal water users, agriculture, and commercial fisheries. It also considers water supply and sewage treatment and some of the alternatives to such treatment. These various matters are grouped together because they all represent *costs* associated with waste disposal which fit, reasonably well, into the market evaluation framework. Conceptually, their inclusion in a cost-minimizing waste-disposal system presents lesser difficulties than public

57

health, aesthetics, or recreation, which are treated in subsequent sections.

For example, treatment costs incurred by an industry, owing to pollution of its intake water, represents a rather clear-cut real cost to society. This cost, under specific circumstances, may or may not be less than other means of dealing with waste disposal such as sewage treatment. The design of cost-minimizing waste-disposal systems clearly requires accurate knowledge of the relations between the significant types of pollution, damages, and/or water-supply treatment costs imposed. In addition, the costs of achieving a range of quality standards for receiving water at specific points of use, by various means, under differing conditions of flow, temperature, etc., must be known. Ideally, a waste-disposal system would equalize all costs (including residual damages) at the margin. Actually, it is unlikely that the relevant types of information will ever be known with ideal accuracy and certainty. *However, there has been comparatively little rigorous analysis of costs from the point of view of designing efficient, interdependent systems.*

Orthodox Sewage Treatment Plants

The character of the relationship between size and costs of relevant types of installations is important information for planning efficient waste-disposal systems. If costs differ with size, the comparative advantage of a unit, in a system, will depend upon the scale that can be efficiently utilized. Partial estimates which have come to the author's attention indicate that there are appreciable economies of scale in the construction and operation of sewage treatment plants.

Studies aimed at isolating and quantifying the relationships between scale of operation and incremental costs, for planning purposes, are a necessary prerequisite to integrated water-quality planning. These studies should, insofar as possible, analyze primary and major types of secondary treatment separately so that the costs of combining the two in various proportions can be inferred. Furthermore, an effort should be made to isolate the major factors that bear upon the transferability of the results to differing situations.

Moreover, the relationship between changes in the rate of operation (i.e., per cent of BOD removal from a given volume of sewage) of particular types of plants and incremental costs (short-run marginal costs) bears investigation. Typically, a sewage treatment plant is designed to maintain a stream oxygen standard at a specified low flow; it is then operated with little or no attention to variations in stream flow.[1] If the standard set for the particular low flow was in some sense correct, unchanged operation of the plant at higher flows may incur unnecessary social costs. Similarly, the design of a cost-minimizing waste-disposal system, which is only partly based on stream standards, may imply variation in the level of plant operation depending upon river stage. Consequently, study to determine the cost savings (if any) which may be achieved by varying degrees of treatment to conform with stream flows is an essential element in waste-disposal cost analysis. Moreover, such study should not be limited to plants as presently designed, since they reflect the objective of continuous rate operation. If the propriety of varying rates of operation is accepted, sewage treatment plants may be likened to a manufacturer operating in a variable market. A plant designed for production in a variable market may be considerably different from one meant to produce at a particular rate. The former is unlikely to achieve as low a level of costs as the latter at its steady rate of output but may well produce at lower cost for rates appreciably higher or lower.[2]

Since municipal and industrial *organic* wastes are ordinarily treated in similar types of plants, analysis of the type sketched above should be applicable to both.

Stabilization Ponds

In the past several years stabilization ponds have drawn extensive attention as treatment devices. In these ponds, putrescible organic sewage wastes are converted into more stable forms, principally living algae. Since the water is quiescent and the area of the air-water interface is comparatively small, oxygen used by the pond's aerobic bacteria, and by the respiration of the algae mass, originates substantially, perhaps principally, in photosynthesis by the algae.

Stabilization ponds initially found application as "polishing" devices for the effluent from secondary treatment plants. In the United States the earliest ponds, meant to serve specifically as secondary or as complete treatment facilities, were constructed in the Northern Great Plains after World War II. In the past few years the use of stabilization ponds

[1] In some instances provision is made for temporary chemical treatment, chlorination of effluent, or lagooning during periods of extreme low flow.

[2] See George Stigler, "Production and Distribution in the Short Run," American Economic Association *Readings in the Theory of Income Distribution* (Philadelphia: The Blakiston Company, 1949), or *Journal of Political Economy,* Vol. 47, June 1939.

has spread rapidly in humid areas, and the Pubilc Health Service has approved a large number for grants under its assistance program. The cost of building stabilization ponds is comparatively low, and they operate dependably with little attention. Many industries in small cities and suburban developments have begun to use them. For large cities, or for industries located in or near urban areas, the relatively great consumption of space by the ponds is a serious disadvantage. However, the utilization of ponds by large cities is not unknown. In Aukland, New Zealand, where the geographical situation is particularly propitious, stabilization ponds serve a population of over a million people, and in Australia large lagoon installations have been found to function efficiently and at low cost.[3]

The place that stabilization ponds can fill in optimum waste-disposal systems remains to be evaluated. A primary factor bearing upon their applicability is the availability and cost of suitable land. While the ponds have generally been viewed as devices for attaining more or less full treatment, they could be operated to attain partial treatment as well. The degree of stabilization achieved as well as the space required, and consequently costs, depends upon the length of detention time in the pond. Study of the comparative costs of stabilization ponds and evaluation of their potential in efficient waste-disposal systems would be of considerable value. This might be done by specifying a prototype basin —modeled to the degree possible on an actual situation—and seeing how stabilization ponds would best combine with other measures. There has been some tendency either to hail the ponds as a panacea or to dismiss their potentialities more or less out of hand.

The study of costs implies that output can be adequately measured. Unfortunately there is a substantial technical impediment to measuring the output (BOD reduction) of stabilization ponds in a manner commensurate with other means of treatment or with dilution. The effluent from a treatment plant contains plant nutrients which will, under propitious conditions, be utilized by algae growth in the receiving water. In a stabilization pond that has reached a situation of biological balance, this step has been essentially completed before the effluent is released. Consequently, a BOD reduction test cannot be performed on a basis comparable with that used for orthodox treatment plants. If the sample is incubated in the dark, death and decay of the algae could result in

[3] C. D. Parker, H. L. Jones, and H. C. Greene, "Performance of Large Sewage Lagoons at Melbourne, Australia," *Sewage and Industrial Wastes,* Vol. 31, No. 2, February 1959. Large lagoon installations give full treatment to sewage from Melbourne, Australia. These installations combine aerobic and anaerobic ponds, which permits higher loadings than aerobic ponds alone.

a higher BOD; if incubated in continuous light, BOD might be negative because of photosynthetic oxygen production.[4]

Does the effluent from stabilization ponds appreciably increase the net amount of algae over long stretches of stream? If so, what is the ultimate effect upon the oxygen balance and other relevant characteristics of the receiving waters? These questions are still to be satisfactorily investigated. The problems here impinge upon those discussed in Chapter V concerning the calculation of assimilative capacity. They reflect the complexity of the receiving-water phenomena and the limited extent to which they are understood.

Harvested Ponds and Tertiary Treatment

Since the algae growth in a stabilization pond may contain almost all of the sewage organics and nutrients, physical removal and disposal of the algae can provide unusually complete separation of unwanted substances from the water. Not only can BOD be drastically reduced, but plant nutrients can be removed as well.[5] Since algae enter into the fish food chain, one way of removing the organic substances from the ponds is by growing and harvesting fish. This technique is, in fact, rather venerable and is used at several locations in Europe and Asia.[6] Fish raised in stabilization ponds are not likely to appeal to the American public, but algae as well as fish harvested from the ponds could be used in animal feeds and in fertilizer.

In addition to providing more complete treatment, harvested ponds can be loaded at a much higher rate than standard stabilization ponds. Research on harvested high-rate oxidation ponds has shown some interesting preliminary results. In California such ponds have been operated with detention periods of 1-3 days. Algae were removed by flocculation

[4] See A. F. Bartsch, "Algae as a Source of Oxygen in Waste Treatment," *Journal, Water Pollution Control Federation*, March 1961, p. 248.

[5] It is reported that algae are capable of reducing nitrogen and phosphorus in effluents by 90 per cent or more. G. P. Fitzgerald and G. A. Rohlich, "An Evaluation of the Stabilization Pond Literature," *Sewage and Industrial Wastes*, October 1958.

[6] See Louis Klein, *Aspects of River Pollution, op. cit.*, p. 448. A detailed discussion of the arrangements at Munich, Germany, is found in Joseph Brix, Karl Imhoff, Robert Weldert, *Die Stadtentwässerung in Deutschland* (Jena: Gustav Fisher Verlag, 1934), pp. 628-43. The Munich fish ponds are capable of higher sewage loads than unharvested stabilization ponds. About two parts dilution water from the river are provided for each part of sewage. At loadings in excess of 1,000 population per acre the ponds are said to produce a high-quality effluent. Professor Gordon Fair informed the author that the ponds are used only during the summer.

or centrifuging. The value of the protein content of the algae cell material for animal feed was reported to be well above the cost of harvesting.[7]

Tertiary treatment aimed specifically at the reduction of plant nutrients in effluents has also been proposed. One form this might take is the growth of algae in a carefully controlled environment, possibly as an additional final stage in standard treatment. It appears reasonable to assume that treatment of this sort (or types of treatment not yet in view but with analogous effects) will find a place in planning waste-disposal systems in areas where plant nutrients cause significant social costs.

Study of the economics of rapid-rate-oxidation ponds and tertiary treatment processes remains to be extended to full-scale units operating under varying conditions. Such investigations must include market analysis for the harvested algae or fish. Study of this kind seems highly important; at this point, methods using algae appear to be the only potentially feasible ones for large-scale removal of plant nutrients.

A possible alternative for dealing with costly or undesirable algae growths is the application of chemical algicides. Several chemical compounds have been demonstrated to have effective (and apparently safe) algicidal properties in ponds. However, dosages have to be determined with care. Moreover, the technical problems, as well as the economics of applying algicides to flowing waters, remain to be evaluated.[8] One advantage of destroying harmful algae growth in the stream is that many plant nutrients enter streams in runoff from fertilized agricultural and residential properties, and thus are not amenable to treatment at waste-water outfalls.

Alterations of and Adaptations to Streamflow Characteristics

Because of the inverse relationship between the concentration of most pollutants and the low-flow stages of streams, the practice of augmenting flow by releases from storage provides a means of relieving pollution during critical periods. Low flows ordinarily coincide

[7] P. H. McGauhey, "Reclamation of Water from Domestic and Industrial Wastes," *Waste Treatment, op. cit.,* p. 440. Quite interestingly a more than 40 per cent reduction in hardness was reported in hard-water sewage from which a large crop of algae was harvested.

[8] For a report on one of the more promising algicides see Thomas E. Maloney, "Control of Algae with Chlorophenyl Dimethyl Urea," *Journal, American Water Works Association,* March 1958, p. 417.

with high temperatures, which depress the oxygen saturation level of receiving waters and increase the toxicity to fish of certain pollutants. Maintaining a given stream condition during periods of natural low flow in heavily loaded streams may often, over certain ranges, exceed the cost of enhancing the flow.

Accordingly flow augmentation is likely to find a place in most optimum waste disposal systems. The comparative advantage of flow augmentation is modified in varying degrees by the fact that it is complementary or competitive with other water uses. Also flow augmentation tends to increase the velocity of flow and hence permits less waste stabilization in a *given stretch* of stream. This is significant for calculation of downstream assimilative capacity, especially if the stream empties into a reservoir or into estuarine waters.

The evaluation of flow augmentation, within the cost minimization framework sketched in earlier sections, implies that the incremental costs of differing amounts of augmentation be adequately determinable. In addition, as in the case of other devices in an interdependent system, its effects on downstream uses must be adequately ascertainable, and the cost functions of alternatives (including pollution damages) must be known, so that the over-all costs of alternative systems that meet the constraints can be explored. Furthermore, the marginal increments or decrements of value, which occur in complementary or competitive uses, must be calculable.

Thus the problems of evaluating flow augmentation are largely those discussed in other parts of this report. However, water released from reservoirs does present some special physical and economic problems requiring further study.[9]

One such problem is the effect of storage on water quality. Some of the results of storage are generally favorable and should add to the comparative advantage of flow augmentation. For example, the chemical and bacteriological quality of water released from impoundment is more stable than that of water flowing regularly in the stream. Furthermore, summer releases tend to be cooler than regular streamflow. On the other hand, some early hopes for the efficacy of dilution through flow augmentation were disappointed because of failure to consider the impact of impoundment upon the dissolved oxygen content of water. Power installations bringing water from deeper parts of

[9] A low-flow augmentation project is under way at Johns Hopkins University and a number of technical problems are under consideration there. See Hull and Carbaugh, *Report No. VI of the Low-Flow Augmentation Project, op. cit.*

reservoirs often emit a flow that is virtually devoid of oxygen.[10] This is due to the combined effect of BOD and reservoir stratification, which may produce a condition of deficient or zero dissolved oxygen in the depths of reservoirs. To achieve a given effect on downstream D.O., larger releases from the reservoir are required and the costs of achieving abatement via dilution are raised. However, methods of dealing with this problem have been devised. For example, air has been successfully introduced into water passing through power turbines. In many installations this can be done comparatively simply by making use of "vacuum breakers" already installed in the dam. Turbine aeration involves some power loss, however, and therefore is not costless.[11] Under some conditions turbine aeration may play an important and economical role in the maintenance of oxygen levels during critical periods, and its potentialities merit careful analysis.

Other methods of reaerating water or preventing reservoir stratification have been suggested and to some extent applied. These include high or multilevel penstock intakes, special tailrace design, compressed air reaeration, and circulation by pumping. The theoretical energy requirement for mixing reservoir water has been calculated and is quite small because of the modest net lift required.[12]

At this point, information is not yet available that will permit an accurate forecast of the comparative cost of achieving a range of D.O. improvement by alternate devices. This type of information is a

[10] See Frederick F. Fish, "Effects of Impoundments on Downstream Water Quality, Roanoke River, North Carolina;" Robert S. Ingols, "Effects of Impoundments on Downstream Water Quality—Catawba River, South Carolina;" and Benjamin H. Hall, Jr., "Reregulation of Impounded Water in Chatahoochee River, Georgia," all in Journal, American Water Works Association, January 1959. The effects of oxygen deficiency in waters released from impoundment may be substantial. Ingols (above, p. 45) makes the following interesting comparison, "By extrapolating the curves of Figure 1 to the dam site, it can be seen that there would be an oxygen deficit of almost 9.0 ppm at the dam. To create this deficit by a sewage BOD, approximately 860,000 people would be required at a flow of 3,300 cfs; at a flow of 13,600 cfs 3,500,000 would be necessary."

[11] A. J. Wiley and B. F. Lueck and R. H. Scott and T. F. Wisniewski, "Commercial Scale Operation of Turbine Aeration on Wisconsin Rivers," Journal, Water Pollution Control Federation, February 1960. The authors state "if firm power is valued at 1¢ per kwh, the cost of aeration by this method appeared to be in the range of $3 to $15 per ton of oxygen absorbed."

In Germany turbine aeration is considered the least expensive means of artificial oxygenation. Friederich Sierp, Gewerbliche und Industriellen Abwässer (Berlin: Springer-Verlag, 1959), p. 68.

[12] G. E. Hutchinson, A Treatise on Limnology, Vol. I, Geography, Physics, and Chemistry (New York: John Wiley and Sons, Inc., 1957) reported in F. W. Kittrell, "Effects of Impoundments on Dissolved Oxygen Resources," Sewage and Industrial Wastes, September 1959.

necessary element in waste-disposal planning and will become progressively more important as many more reservoirs are built for multi-purpose flow regulation.[13]

The operation of reservoirs does not necessarily have a favorable effect on the assimilative capacity of streams, even when viewed solely with respect to the volume of streamflow or dilution capacity. The use of power dams for "peaking" often results in a streamflow that is less favorable to waste disposal than the natural flow. In some instances, changes in operating procedure or reregulation by means of small control structures downstream may merit consideration as economical control devices. The potentialities and costs of reregulation for pollution abatement have been relatively little explored but they appear to be considerable.[14] Thus far, reregulation has found its primary application in augmenting low flows in support of navigation and power.

An alternative method of utilizing the dilution potentialities of streamflow is the temporary lagooning of wastes. It is axiomatic that under some conditions it would be less expensive to "store the wastes than to store the river" but comparatively little is known about the over-all potentialities of this technique. Since even small impoundments consume a relatively large space, much depends upon the cost and availability of suitably located land. The feasibility of industrial applications, in which the greatest potentialities lie, depends largely upon the location of industrial plants with respect to heavily populated areas with high land value. The studies of individual heavy water-using industries that are suggested subsequently should include an evaluation of the feasibility of temporary lagooning, as well as of stabilization ponds.

Temporary lagooning would have advantages aside from its role in co-ordinating waste discharges with streamflow. If the retention period is significantly long, the lagoons will partially stabilize the wastes in the manner of stabilization ponds. In addition, temporary storage would help prevent accidental "spills" and the hazards they entail. "Spills" occur for a variety of reasons including leaks or breaks in lines, accidental opening of valves, and treatment plant failures. In a river basin where there has been considerable experience with such spills, it may be possible to compute the mathematical probability of at

[13] See, for example, the projections of storage increments in Senate Select Committee on Water Resources, Committee Print No. 32, p. 68.

[14] See Benjamin H. Hall, Jr., "Reregulation of Impounded Water, Chatahoochee River, Georgia," *op. cit.* Professor C. J. Velz of the School of Public Health, University of Michigan, has also stressed the importance and applicability of this technique in numerous writings and in conversation with the author.

least part of the damages and use this information in the design of
efficient systems for waste disposal and water supply.[15] A possible disadvantage of the co-ordination of sewage releases with streamflow is that
it would tend to diminish volume during periods of low flow and increase it during higher flows. This might well be a fatal defect in arid
areas. Relatively little systematic information is available on any of
these matters.

It is notable that the comparative advantage of techniques that alter
streamflow, or conform waste releases to flow, depends upon the
specific character of the streamflow pattern or hydrograph, not just
upon low flow. Thus, relative costs will differ from situation to situation not only because loads, land values, and construction costs differ,
but also because the natural pattern of flow differs. In general, the less
variable the flow the less the comparative advantage of these techniques.

A partial alternative to temporary lagooning or flow augmentation
would be temporary shutdown of industrial plants with heavy waste
loads during extreme low flows. It is possible to imagine that this
might be an efficient supplement to other methods, especially with
respect to industries that can accumulate inventories, but it would be
very difficult to implement under the U.S. system of laws and institutions.

A final and highly important point about all techniques that call
upon the variable dilution capability of stream flows is that their value
may be modified by the effects of residual wastes upon lakes and
estuaries. The increase of pollutants, especially in the form of plant
nutrients, in lakes has become a source of concern to some students.
This arises from observation of changes which have taken place in
American and Swiss lakes. During the past fifty years, a number of
lakes have shown striking changes in flora and fauna—generally to the
detriment of the higher qualities of fish.[16] The extensive, recently
initiated, study of the Great Lakes by the U.S. Public Health Service

[15] Spills are surprisingly frequent along the heavily industralized Ohio. See
Chronicle of the Twelfth Year, Ohio River Valley Water Sanitation Commission,
Cincinnati, Ohio, December 1, 1960.
[16] Most of the world's research on the biochemistry of lakes has been done
in Switzerland. See O. Jaag (Director of the Federal Institute for Water Supply,
Sewage Purification and Water Pollution Control, Swiss Federal Institute of
Technology, Zurich), "The Pollution of Surface and Ground Waters in Switzerland," *Water Pollution in Europe,* Fourth European Seminar for Sanitary Engineers (Geneva: World Health Organization, 1956), pp. 113 ff.

should help to shed light upon the significance of such problems in the United States. Also, since the primary impacts of lake pollution appear to be on recreation and commercial fisheries, general studies in those areas, as outlined subsequently, should help to delineate the social costs involved.

Tidal estuaries and bays are the final recipients, prior to discharge into the oceans, of all residual waterborne wastes. Moreover, they often directly receive large waste loads from the extensive economic and demographic development along their shores. The estuaries have been called ". . . unquestionably the most complex aquatic environments in the entire world. . . ."[17]

The many influences that operate in estuaries greatly increase the technical difficulties of forecasting concentration of pollutants, and their effects. For many years the analysis of estuarine waste dilution and waste transport to the ocean was based on the concept of the tidal "prism." In recent years it has become clear that retention periods are often much longer than was implied by the prism theory, and more complex analytical techniques have been proposed. At the present time there is no standard analysis.[18]

Estuarine pollution is extensive in Europe as well as in the United States. In both areas its major impacts appear to be upon aesthetics, recreation, and commercial fishing (particularly shell fishing). In some instances estuarine pollution has affected fishing indirectly, as well as directly, by blocking the way of ocean fish that spawn in fresh water. However, the vicissitudes of nature, as well as heavy fishing, so profoundly affect the quality of fishing grounds that there is considerable difficulty in distinguishing actual causalty from *post hoc, ergo propter hoc* reasoning in this field.[19]

[17] Thurlow C. Nelson, "Some Aspects of Pollution, Parasitism, and Inlet Restriction in Three New Jersey Estuaries," *Biological Problems in Water Pollution, Transactions of the 1959 Seminar,* U.S. Department of Health, Education, and Welfare, Public Health Service, Robert A. Taft Sanitary Engineering Center Technical Report W60-3, Cincinnati, 1960.

[18] "The field of sanitary engineering offers no question more profound than the following: 'What is the fate of a particle of waste discharged into a mass of tidal water?'" H. G. Hanson and Bernard B. Berger, "Where Does Research Stand in Water Pollution Control?" *Journal, Water Pollution Control Federation,* May 1961, p. 482.

[19] In 1949 the oil industry on the Gulf of Mexico was sued for approximately $40 million, the largest civil suit ever filed in the United States up to that time. A very extensive investigation followed. The trouble affecting the oyster beds was found to be a parasitic organism. See Gordon Gunter, "Pollution Problems Along the Gulf Coast," *Biological Problems in Water Pollution, op. cit.*

In instances where estuarine pollution is destructive, flow augmentation or co-ordinated release of wastes in streams emptying into the estuary do not mitigate the situation. Indeed, it is possible for both measures to increase estuarine pollution by accelerating the carriage of unassimilated wastes into the estuary.[20] Thus the value of treatment as contrasted to dilution may be enhanced when effects on estuaries or bays are considered. However, to the degree that plant nutrient problems are involved, orthodox treatment may not substantially ameliorate the situation either. In that instance, tertiary treatment (not yet operational) or other means of disposal not involving the delivery of wastes to fresh-water resources would have great merit.[21]

The studies of recreation and fisheries recommended subsequently should help to give perspective to some of the significant economic variables involved in the pollution of estuaries. But, much better understanding of physical and biological factors is required as well, before efficient waste disposal systems can be designed in basins that significantly influence the quality of estuarine waters.

Municipal Water Supply—Damage and Treatment Costs

While the major objective in public water supply treatment is the preservation of public health, other objectives can also involve significant social costs. Hardness, acidity, alkalinity, chlorides, and tastes and odors usually do not represent a threat to public health but may erode equipment, increase soap usage, induce the purchase or rental of water softeners and/or bottled water, and be destructive to plant life. These are social costs, and to the degree that they result from pollution they should enter into cost minimization analysis. No careful, detailed, and comprehensive study has been made of the costs that various pollutants over a range of concentrations impose upon municipal users.

When such a study is made, care must be exercised that all relevant aspects of quality change are included in the calculations. Conflicts, for example, may arise from the differing quality requirements of various uses or users. Softening of public supplies can achieve some

[20] See Interstate Commission on the Delaware Basin, *Dispersion Studies on the Delaware River Estuary Model and Potential Applications Toward Stream Purification Capacity Evaluation,* June 1961, pp. 11-12.

[21] In the case of cities or industries located on estuaries or bays, the barging of some wastes to sea may be part of an efficient feasible solution. See Bostwick H. Ketchum, "Marine Pollution Problems in the North Atlantic Area," *Biological Problems in Water Pollution, op. cit.,* pp. 212 ff.

economies in the use of soap and in avoided scale formation, but the ion exchange processes that substitute sodium for calcium may make the water less suitable for people on a low-sodium diet. In addition, scale formed by a moderate amount of calcium tends to reduce corrosion in pipes and equipment. Similarly, the reduction of water supply temperatures, which improves water as a coolant, increases the cost of heating it. About 30 per cent of the water used for domestic purposes is heated.[22]

Analysis of the costs of making various desirable changes in raw water polluted in varying degrees is also necessary if the social costs of waste disposal are to be minimized. Much information of a relevant character no doubt exists as a result of numerous engineering design studies. There is need, however, for the data available to be extended and brought together in a systematic fashion. Information should be provided that would permit the transferability of the cost estimates to be judged. One of the more important results of this type of analysis would be an indication of the sensitivity of treatment costs to various types of pollutants (including those caused indirectly, through algae growth, for example).

Direct Recirculation

While direct recirculation of treated municipal sewage for public water supplies has occurred only in conditions of extreme stringency, under some circumstances it might present an economical alternative to the usual practices.[23] For example, a stream used primarily for industrial waste disposal might present more difficult treatment problems than a city's sewage effluent. However, there are always alternative

[22] Jack Hirschleifer, James C. De Haven, and Jerome Milliman, *Water Supply: Economics, Technology, and Policy* (Chicago: University of Chicago Press, 1960), p. 200.

[23] The most widely known instance of recirculation in the United States occurred in Chanute, Kansas, during the winter of 1956-57. Sewage was also reused for all municipal purposes by Lyndon, Kansas, in the fall of 1956, when the normal water supply was exhausted. Ottumwa, Iowa, faced what amounted to a reuse problem, in some respects more difficult than that of the other cities, when about 60 per cent of the flow in the Des Moines River, the supply source, consisted of septic raw sewage, discharged by the city of Des Moines. See Bernard B. Berger, "Public Health Aspects of Water Reuse for Potable Supply," *Journal, American Water Works Association,* Vol. 52, No. 5, May 1960, pp. 599 ff. In the special circumstances of cities which otherwise discharge effluents into the ocean or other places from which they cannot be reclaimed recirculation would constitute a net saving of water.

sources of supply—underground water and transportation of water from other locations, for example. The comparative costs of all relevant alternatives including recirculation would have to be considered in order to design the most efficient system for waste disposal and water supply. It is possible to imagine situations in which partial or complete recirculation would be indicated. This is, however, an area where emotions are notoriously involved, and society might prefer to avoid direct recirculation even though treatment resulted in "safe" supplies. Here, cost analysis would be confined to the role of indicating what the aesthetic differences must "at least" be worth.

Experience with recirculation in Chanute, Kansas, and other evidence, indicates that the potentially most costly aspect of recirculation is the control of dissolved solids. Estimates of the average buildup of dissolved salts to be expected from a single round of domestic sewage run about 100 ppm.[24] In Chanute, where water was recirculated eight to fifteen times during a period of five months, a considerable buildup of chlorides occurred, while the coliform index was successfully maintained at a "safe level" by such orthodox means as chlorination, coagulation, long sedimentation, filtration, and post chlorination.[25]

Thus it appears that a combination of current standard sewage and water treatment processes would have to be supplemented in order to permit continuous recirculation for potable supplies. However, treatment processes could be devised that would continuously produce potable water supplies from sewage at lesser costs than would be involved in an alternative procedure such as the conversion of sea water. Dissolved solids are much lower in sewage effluent so that ion-exchange membrane processes or electrodialysis could be employed efficiently. Technical problems, such as clogging of membranes due to organic materials in the effluent, do exist. Nevertheless, public water supplies might be produced at costs below those of some of the more

[24] Senate Select Committee on National Water Resources Print No. 30, March 1960, p. 25. The alkyl-benzene-sulfonate concentration also built up to undesirable levels.

[25] The experience at Chanute did not actually constitute a case of direct recirculation of the treatment plant effluent, since the impoundment into which the effluent was discharged and from which the public supply was drawn acted as a stabilization pond. See Dwight Metzler, Russel Culp, et al., *Journal, American Water Works Association*, August 1958, p. 1021. The authors noted, however, the low efficiency of the water treatment process in reducing the number of plankton, free-living amoebae and their cysts, and other free-living organisms. The public health significance of these organisms is that they harbor bacteria and protect them from chlorination.

spectacular conveyance schemes. Moreover, partial rather than complete recirculation could help ease the burden on treatment facilities. Some effluent might be continuously discharged and replaced with fresh make-up water.

It does not appear that direct recirculation for potable supplies would soon enter into a cost-minimizing waste-disposal system having constraints based upon public health considerations, except perhaps in unusual circumstances. However, if this is the case, it appears even less likely that the conversion of sea water would be an alternative in an optimal system. While some analysis of comparative costs has been made,[26] careful study, taking as its point of departure optimal system design, could perform a constructive job of clarification in an area where emotional appeal has been rampant.

The use of a distribution system for potable supplies, separate from the one that provides water for general municipal uses, has often been proposed. With respect to recirculation, this might mean that a comparatively small proportion of the water supply would be treated to the high standards of purity demanded for drinking water (perhaps it would even be distilled), while the remainder would be recirculated with less extensive treatment. Alternatively a fresh supply (presumably limited in amount or expensive to tap) could be used for potable supplies, while the treated effluent is recirculated for general municipal uses. The fresh potable supply could serve as make-up water to prevent the building up of dissolved solids in the recirculated portion. Other combinations utilizing a separate circulation system for municipal supplies could be organized. Public health authorities have generally been critical of plans of this character because of the dangers involved in accidental cross connections or deliberate use of the non-potable supplies for human ingestion. Despite these risks, plans utilizing separate systems merit cost analysis so that society can weigh possible savings and/or better, or more pleasing, drinking water supplies against the risks involved.[27]

Ground water recharge is an alternative way of making treated sewage available for general reuse. This can be accomplished by means of injection wells or spreading grounds.

The spreading technique (as contrasted to injection wells) has the advantage of purifying the water to some extent before it enters the

---

[26] Abel Wolman, "Impact of Desalinization on the Water Economy," *Journal, American Water Works Association,* Vol. 53, February 1961, p. 119.

[27] These dangers can be mitigated by chlorinating the recirculated supply.

water-bearing strata, or alternatively of requiring less treatment than water injected through wells. The purification process in the soil occurs predominantly during passage through the unsaturated zone and results from the action of soil bacteria, filtration, adsorption, and perhaps other processes.[28] In parts of the arid West or Southwest where spreading grounds are available at convenient locations, it is possible that a major share of treated domestic sewage effluents could be economically and productively utilized in this manner. Evaluation of this method on a basis comparable with alternative measures presents formidable difficulties, but effort in this direction is merited because of the apparent potential of the technique in some areas.[29]

Industry Studies

A number of industries use copious amounts of water for cooling and process purposes. In the United States as a whole about twice as much

[28] Based on a comment by Bernard B. Berger, Head of Pollution Control and Water Supply Research, Taft Sanitary Engineering Center, Cincinnati, Ohio. If passage through the unsaturated zone proved capable of reducing the content of chemicals to an appreciable degree, the advantage might be particularly great. Although studies indicate that bacteria travel only short distances in ground waters, it is known that chemicals may be transported considerable distances. See P. H. McGauhey, "Water Reclamation from Liquid Wastes," *Water Treatment, op. cit.,* p. 437.

Recharge of ground water supplies for municipal use has been practiced in Germany for many years. The recharge water is obtained from the heavily polluted rivers, and recharge is accomplished in such a way that the water filters through the ground. See Gordon M. Fair, "Pollution Abatement in the Ruhr District," *Comparisons in Resource Management* (Baltimore: Johns Hopkins Press, December 1961).

[29] Caution in the use of reclaimed sewage for recharge is in order because ground-water contamination presents somewhat special problems. Such contamination tends to be persistent, and a significant amount of ground water is used directly for potable supplies without previous treatment. The problems of ground-water contamination have recently been highlighted by the widespread discovery of alkyl-benzene-sulfonate in well waters, largely attributable to the use of septic tanks in housing developments. Graham Walton, "ABS Contamination of Water Resources," *Journal, American Water Works Association,* Vol. 52, No. 11, November 1960. The septic tank and tile disposal field type of installation presently serves over 17 million homes in the United States. See Senate Select Committee Reprint No. 30, March 1960. While the concentrations thus far found could not be considered health hazards, the situation is not entirely comfortable because of potential increases in concentrations and the fact that ABS may indicate the presence of other, possibly more deleterious components of domestic sewage. Careful checking of water used for recharge would be mandatory to avoid the accidental contamination of underground supplies.

water is withdrawn by manufacturing industries as by municipalities. Steam power plants withdraw over twice as much water as all other industries combined, almost all of which is for cooling. Water withdrawals by all industries for processing alone are somewhat less than total municipal withdrawals. The contribution of industry to over-all oxygen-demanding pollution loadings is not precisely known but is thought to be well over half the total, neglecting the effects of heat pollution on the oxygen balance of receiving waters. In addition, industry expels large amounts of inorganic and persistent organic materials.

While damages to industrial equipment, industrial water treatment costs, and the treatment of various types of industrial wastes represent some of the more clear-cut social costs of waste disposal, remarkably little precise information is available about them. This results from both the reluctance of industry to divulge exact figures and the inherent complexity of the problem. Each industrial plant is in some significant respects in a class by itself. Consequently, generalization is difficult.

This reflects the fact that there are a wide variety of ways in which industry can respond to water and waste water problems. For example, recirculation of cooling water, and to some degree process water, is a fact in many industries. Changes in processes that result in the reclamation of what otherwise would be waste materials may accompany recirculation or be a partial or complete substitute for effluent treatment. Moreover, changes in process, affecting pollution loads, are made in response to a variety of considerations only one of which may be waste-disposal problems.

While the numerous ways in which industry copes with its water environment are encouraging in that they indicate adaptability to a wide variety of conditions, they present difficulties for the identification and prediction of the social costs of pollution. Perhaps the most fruitful approach for research would be intensive study of each of the major water-using and polluting industries in terms of its over-all, interrelated effects on, and responses to, the water resources environment. These relationships can be classified into three elements. First, the withdrawal of water from the water source. Second, water depletion by evaporation or incorporation in the product. Finally, the quality characteristics of the water returned to the stream. Each element is capable of variation within technically defined limits, and variation of one element tends to be reflected in the others.

Studies of these elements should provide systematic information concerning pollution loadings, pollution damages, and methods and costs of water and sewage treatment. This would help to identify the scope for process changes and waste reclamation as alternatives to the treatment of waste water. It is notable that while process changes and/or reclamation of wastes may not be economically justifiable when the alternative is (apparently) costless waste disposal, they may often involve relatively less net cost than waste treatment or other means of attaining optimum reduction in waste delivered to a stream and therefore find a place in an efficient system. Among the methods that might be useful in making the proposed studies is cross-section type comparison and analysis of plants in different regions presenting a variety of water resources environments. Such studies could also yield useful information about the influence of water resources on plant location.

Technological-economic-locational analysis of each of the major industries that uses water and produces waste water would yield information not only on current cost relationships but on other matters related to the design of optimal waste-disposal systems and the evaluation of emerging water resources problems. Knowledge of technological tendencies and responses to conditioning factors is not only essential for planning waste-disposal systems, but would be helpful in making overall projections of various aspects of national and regional water demand including the demand for pollution abatement. For example, some students of pollution problems believe that the waste materials produced per unit of output in a number of important industries have been falling substantially in recent years because of recirculation and other process changes; and that consequently projections of waste loadings based on invariant relationships are likely to be wide of the mark.[30]

Furthermore, a close study of production processes and the cost of technical alternatives would aid in predicting responses to public policy and other environmental changes. In Part I, where the example of a basin-wide firm was used to illustrate the character of an optimal waste disposal system, it was assumed that municipal water rates would be set equal to the full marginal cost of making the supply available. However, it has recently been argued that water prices in practice are gen-

---

[30] Abel Wolman (Chairman, Department of Sanitary Engineering, Johns Hopkins University) expressed this opinion in conversation with the author. See also the paper by Leonard E. Pasek, *The Needs and Obligations of Industry*, U.S. Department of Health, Education and Welfare, National Conference on Water Pollution, Sheraton-Park Hotel, Washington, D.C., December 12-14, 1960. The possibility of reducing industrial pollution loadings by recirculation (and attendant treatment) is also stressed in Friederich Sierp, *Gwerbliche und Industrielle Abwässer* (Berlin: Springer-Verlag, 1959), p. 81.

erally too low.[31] Furthermore the cost of obtaining a given quantity and quality of water may be expected to rise in the future.[32] To the degree that water costs affect recirculation and attendant treatment, they may also affect waste loads. The suggested studies should help to reveal the effects of increased water costs not only on water intake, but upon depletion and waste loadings as well.

Damages to Commercial Fisheries

The effects of pollution on commercial and sport fisheries may be substantial, but they are not always destructive. A modest amount of organic pollution can stimulate algae growth and thus increase the productivity of fisheries. On the other hand, toxic materials, oxygen depletion, temperature changes, and excessive or toxic algae growth can reduce the amount of fish life and alter its character. Often the major effect of pollution is to reduce the number of valuable fish while coarser types flourish. Some students of the Great Lakes feel, for example, that the increased volume but reduced value of the fish catch there is a result of changes brought about largely by pollution.[33]

Damage to commercial fisheries can, of course, quite manifestly be a social cost of pollution but its character is often misunderstood.[34] To take an extreme example, suppose that commercial fishing is

[31] See Hirschleifer *et al.*, *Water Supply, op. cit.*, pp. 43-47. Interestingly the same point has been stressed with respect to Germany by Siegfried Balke, Minister for Atomic Energy and Water Economics. See "Reinhaltung des Wassers als Investitions—Problem," *Der Stadtetag*, Vol. 6, 1960, W. Kohlhammer Verlag, Stuttgart.

[32] For an analysis of this point, set Irving Fox, "Water: Supply, Demand and the Law," *Rocky Mountain Law Review*, University of Colorado, June 1960, p. 457.

[33] Professors Chandler and Ayer of the Great Lakes Institute, University of Michigan, Ann Arbor, in conversation with the author.

[34] For example, a recent Soviet publication has put the damages of pollution in the Soviet Union at 3 billion rubles of which almost one-half is attributed to losses of commercial fish. From a national point of view this loss is probably overstated in the manner subsequently explained in the text. On the other hand, it does indicate that extensive pollution problems exist in the Soviet Union. From Gusev, A. G., "Zagriaznenie Rybokhoziaistvennykh Vodoemov Stochnymi Vodami i Ushcherb, Nanosimyi Imi Rybnoi Promyshlenosti," Iz-va M-va Sel'skogo Khoziaistva, SSSR, Moskva 1957 (Pollution of Soviet Fishing Streams and Consequent Losses to the Fishing Industry). Citation and translation provided by Michael Gucovsky. Other European nations also report large losses suffered by commercial fisheries, see, for example, "Bekämpfung de Gewässerchmutzung" *Bulletin Des Presse und Informationsamptes der Bundesregierung Bonn*, January 28, 1961, p. 179.

brought to a complete halt in a given area and that the market value of the catch was formerly $1 million. The loss to the nation is not $1 million but that amount minus the value of the transferable resources which were released by the cessation of fishing and which can now be shifted to other activities. Where the value of the catch is reduced by the destruction of the more valuable fish, the computations are more complicated but the principle is the same. Needless to say, the loss calculated as indicated above is clearly a net economic loss.

In the United States the primary areas where losses of commercial fisheries due to pollution can occur are in lakes (mostly the Great Lakes) and in coastal waters. As already noted, these waters present some of the most difficult technical problems encountered in the investigation of physical aspects of pollution. In regard to the Great Lakes, for example, views differ on the extent to which notable changes already observed in aquatic life are attributable to pollution, to other activities of various kinds (fishing, for example) or to long-term natural changes.

These factors make the accurate determination of damages to commercial fisheries extremely difficult. One, possibly helpful approach would be to select a body of water in which commercial fishing has clearly been damaged by pollution, if such can be identified, and attempt to estimate the net return (positive or negative) attainable by reducing waste loads in varying degrees. This would require projections of fishing quality, value of catch, and investment and operating costs. Such an analysis would have to rest in considerable measure upon conjecture, but it might help to indicate the degree to which the net damages (or real cost) of foregone fishing opportunities can help to justify a pollution abatement program. Ideally, for purposes of devising optimum waste-disposal systems, net losses and net returns should be known as functions of various types and amounts of pollution.

Agriculture and Pollution Costs

It is well known that evapotranspiration and leaching cause the salinity of streams that are heavily used for irrigation to rise in the course of their flow. Along certain streams in the arid Southwest, such as the Rio Grande and the Pecos, salinity at times rises to levels that seriously impair utility of the water. A high level of salinity in water is very destructive to a number of industrial processes, it reduces the suitability of water for municipal supplies, and treatment is a costly process. Downstream agriculture is also inhibited, and the amount of water applied per acre tends to rise. Conversely, industrial pollution can destroy irrigated crops and make water supplies unsuitable for consumption by cattle.

Recent decades have shown not only a strong movement of industry westward, but a tendency for irrigation to move East. Supplementary irrigation of crops has grown particularly rapidly in the Middle West and in the past several years has appeared throughout almost the entire Eastern United States. As more land is put under irrigation in the East, salinity problems may be expected to appear, and conflicts with industrial waste disposal will tend to become more frequent.[35]

No study has been focused explicitly upon the present and potential place of agriculture in pollution problems. Systematic information on the effect of irrigation upon water quality and the costs imposed upon agriculture by industrial pollution would be an important aid to river basin planning, especially in areas where irrigation is already an important activity. The water-quality management study of the Colorado River Basin now under way by the Public Health Service, points to the need for research on the effects of irrigation on dissolved solids, particularly chlorides, in those instances where return flow from irrigation constitutes a major portion of low flow in streams.[36]

AESTHETICS AND RECREATION

For aesthetic reasons, if for no others, most people seem to feel that extreme nuisance conditions are to be avoided in all bodies of water to which the public is exposed. Thus, agreement may probably be assumed that such waters are to be kept in an aerobic condition and that unsightly floating or suspended matter is to be avoided. Beyond

[35] Some instances of such conflicts are already reported. See A. Allan Schmid, *Michigan Water Use and Development Problems,* Circular Bulletin 230 1961, Agricultural Experiment Station, Department of Agricultural Economics, Michigan State University, East Lansing, p. 13, see also Harold H. Ellis, "Some Legal Aspects of Water Use in North Carolina," in *The Law of Water Allocation in the Eastern U.S.,* The Conservation Foundation, Inc., New York, 1958, pp. 215-218, and pp. 301-305, and Mark E. Borton and Harold H. Ellis, *Some Legal Aspects of Water Use in Louisiana,* Bulletin No. 537, Louisiana State University and Agricultural and Mechanical College, June 1960, pp. 24-28.

[36] Kenneth C. Nobe, Project Economist, Colorado River Basin Water Quality Control Project, U.S. Public Health Service, Department of Health, Education, and Welfare. Information provided in correspondence with the author.

these basic points, however, opinion may well differ. The aesthetic and recreational attraction of streams or lakes may be increased by reducing turbidity, confining algae growth, providing a hospitable environment for fish, and by maintaining safe conditions for swimming or boating. To the degree that a body of water provides general aesthetic and environmental satisfactions, it is a collective good which it is virtually impossible to evaluate on the basis of concepts derived from individualistic welfare economics.[37] As pointed out in Part I, this means that such effects cannot be integrally included in a cost minimization analysis. Rather, a basis must be found for achieving political agreement on standards that will be viewed as limits on the cost minimization objective.

However, it appears that the costs of destroying strictly recreational values can, at least in principle, be adequately imputed from individual valuations. Any systematic private undervaluation of recreation, from a social point of view, would more legitimately be compensated by a subsidy to all recognizably beneficial forms of recreation than by attributing special benefits to particular types.[38]

It is important that methods of valuation be developed since the costs of maintaining bodies of water for recreational purposes will be one of the (perhaps the) major expenses of future pollution abatement programs. Unlike diversion uses, the value of water for recreation depends upon its quality *in situ*. Consequently, for this purpose water-supply treatment or related measures cannot be substituted for pollution abatement over certain ranges.

When valuation of recreation is attempted, consistency with consumer sovereignty demands that it be done with the recognition that different forms of recreation may be highly substitutable at the margin and without arbitrary (for insufficiently substantiated) judgments concerning the value of water-based recreation compared with other forms of consumption. Since more intensive future multiple use of streams will entail the construction of reservoir storage for regulation purposes, an important issue will be the rate at which consumers are willing to substitute reservoir-based for stream-based recreation.

A highly ingenious preliminary effort to measure the demand for

[37] For a lucid discussion of what is involved see Richard A. Musgrave, *The Theory of Public Finance* (New York: McGraw-Hill Book Company, 1959), pp. 9-13.

[38] A somewhat analogous distinction was made by Edward S. Mason in regard to conserving individual resources as contrasted to broad resource categories. See "The Political Economy of Resource Use," in Henry Jarrett, editor, *Perspectives on Conservation* (Baltimore: Johns Hopkins Press, 1958), p. 158.

outdoor recreation has already been made.[39] Further work along these lines is of the first order of importance.

Special attention should be directed toward developing methodologies for determination of demand functions for separate categories of water-based recreation such as fishing, swimming, and boating. The nature of pollution is such that opportunities for one or more of these can often be preserved while others are destroyed. Since the demand for recreation has been growing rapidly in recent years, the identification of specific demand functions would merely be a first step in the provision of adequate information for planning purposes. Means would have to be found for projecting the shifts in such functions as well.

Since it may be a long while before the real cost of recreation opportunities foregone can be satisfactorily estimated, social cost minimization may have to be carried on within the constraint of standards set to preserve or enhance the recreation value of all or selected waters. The most rigorous standards (except bacterial) would in general be applicable to fishing waters. Setting such standards is a complex and difficult problem, but reasonably satisfactory ones can probably be devised to achieve given objectives. Some criteria will apply over comparatively wide areas—temperature, D.O. and pH for example. For plant nutrients and toxicants a tailor-made approach utilizing bioassays may be required.[40]

As explained previously, testing the cost of maintaining standards set in this way can indicate what the recreational opportunities afforded must "at least" be worth. Moreover, this process can be refined by testing the cost implication of various zoning possibilities. The significance of the application of computer procedures to the physical and economic data involved in making such comparisons has already been indicated.

PUBLIC HEALTH

In Part I it was contended that some aspects of public health defy evaluation by techniques based upon market concepts. The interdependencies characteristic of infectious disease nullify the social rationale of individual market valuations. Moreover, except for the

[39] See Marion Clawson, *Methods of Measuring the Demand for and Value of Outdoor Recreation* (Washington, D.C.: Resources for the Future, Inc., 1959).
[40] See Clarence M. Tarzwell, "Water Quality Criteria for Aquatic Life," *Transactions of the Seminar on Biological Problems in Water Pollution*, Robert A. Taft Sanitary Engineering Center, Cincinnati, Ohio, 1960.

presumably rare misanthrope, people simply appear to prefer living
in a society where they are not regularly confronted with the spectacle
of mass illness.[41] Consequently society may wish to impose health
standards higher than those a substantial segment of the population
would freely be willing to pay for.

Some of the effects of illness upon over-all income could conceivably be measured. It is not difficult to imagine situations in which
an increment in national product (reduced real cost of waste disposal)
could easily justify the installation of water-treatment facilities without
regard to the more subtle aspects of the problem. Thus, some degree
of water treatment—primarily chlorination—can surely be justified
solely on economic grounds. The working time lost because of, as well
as the resources consumed in the treatment of, diseases such as typhoid,
cholera, and dysentery could easily involve huge social costs.

However, the urban population of the United States apparently has
chosen to set standards of water treatment sufficiently high to avoid any
substantial possibility of epidemic. These standards, while not offering
perfect protection, are probably beyond what could be justified simply
on the basis of enhanced production. Cases of infectious disease resulting from water withdrawn from public water supply systems using
modern treatment methods are practically unknown. The few that can
definitely be traced to water supplies are the results of breakdown,
or of improper operation.[42] Consequently, present bacteriological
standards may properly be viewed as reflecting an attitude toward
disease not based upon the maximization of economic return. Conceivably it could be demonstrated that some lowering of such standards would release resources permitting an over-all increase in the
market value of production. Action based on such a demonstration
might, however, neglect important public values.

Thus, accepting for the moment some prevailing water supply standard, it is still necessary to face the difficult but important question of
whether stream standards must support the water supply standard, and,

---

[41] For a discussion of deficiencies of various proposals to set a value on human
life, see Charles J. Hitch and Roland N. McKean, *The Economics of Defense
in the Nuclear Age* (Cambridge: Harvard University Press, 1960), p. 185 ff.

[42] The most spectacular case of an outbreak of water-borne disease in a city
having modern treatment facilities is an infectious hepatitis epidemic which
occurred in New Delhi, India, in 1955-56. There is, however, much skepticism
about the effectiveness with which the treatment plant was operated. For a discussion of the episode see Bernard B. Berger, "Public Health Aspects of Water
Reuse for Potable Supply," *Journal, American Water Works Association*, Vol. 52,
No. 5, May 1960, p. 601.

if so, what they should be. The answer is obviously of some moment for the design of efficient systems for waste disposal and water supply. Presuming that public health aspects of bathing and other activities involving contact with raw water could be neglected, the sole economic problem would be that of determining the lowest cost method of achieving desired water quality at the tap. This might or might not involve sewage treatment and chlorination of sewage effluent. Since coliform bacteria die off rather quickly in a body of water and since all waters—including those heavily loaded with pollutants—have some self-purification powers, it appears that simple cost minimization would give major weight to water supply treatment, as opposed to sewage treatment. However, some difficulties are involved in biological treatment of unassimilated wastes in highly dilute form, should that be required, and possibilities of system failure may have to be taken into account. Consequently, some quality requirements may have to be placed on raw water ultimately intended for potable supplies. On the other hand, where waters are used for bathing, bacteriological standards set for that purpose would probably dominate the raw water limit set for public supplies. Similarly, in waters used for sport fishing, D.O. requirements of the fish would probably dominate drinking water requirements. Among the major unresolved issues having a bearing upon the character of such standards is the capacity of water supply treatment to deal with bacteriological contamination. Experience over the years has indicated that public water supply treatment systems are capable of handling much heavier bacteriological loads than was long supposed.

Bacteriological contamination, the classic public health consideration, is in some respects simpler to define and deal with than are the health problems presented by some other pollutants. Standard inorganic poisons and a limited range of highly toxic organic materials have been studied for some time by Public Health authorities, and tolerance levels have been set.[43] These tolerances are based primarily on acute toxicity tests and large safety margins. Even with respect to the standard poisons, there is considerable doubt concerning the specific character of chronic effects on humans. Nevertheless, the existing standards could serve, at least initially, as constraints or limits in the cost-minimization analysis of systems. In the case of these poisons, standards for

[43] See M. B. Ettinger, "Proposed Toxicity Screening Procedures for Use in Protecting Drinking Water Quality," *Journal, American Water Works Association,* Vol. 52, No. 6, June 1960.

potable supplies can probably be translated into raw-water standards in a comparatively straightforward fashion because of the limited ability of present water supply treatment plants to deal with them. In fishing streams, standards set to safeguard that purpose may dominate public health limits. In most instances the only effective way to eliminate dangerous concentration of these toxic substances is segregation and treatment or special disposal at the source.

More intractable difficulties are posed by the vast number of synthetic organic chemicals produced by modern industry. Over 500,000 have been synthesized, and a substantial and variable number are found in low concentration in waters used as a source of public drinking water supplies.[44] Standard water-supply treatment methods often have little effect on them. The possibility that these chemicals, even in very low concentration, may have chronic pathological effects on humans is of concern to public health authorities. The presence of toxic materials in water is particularly significant because total human ingestion of water far exceeds that of all solids. The magnitude of the task involved in determining the chronic pathological effects of all, or even a substantial portion, of these compounds is impossibly large under current circumstances. It has been estimated that fewer than 100 qualified toxicologists are now working in the United States.[45] The scarcity of qualified personnel plus the complexity of tracing chronic, including possible reproductive, effects of chemical compounds on mammals means that the cost involved in testing a single compound is very high. Estimates running from $50,000 to $500,000 per compound have been reported by manufacturers required to demonstrate the safety of food additives and drugs.[46] In addition there are serious conceptual problems involved in testing chemicals on a "one at a time" basis under laboratory conditions. For one thing, association with other chemicals in a body of water, as well as subjection to bacterial metabolism, may cause a com-

[44] An interesting set of techniques has also been proposed for deducing drinking water standards from other toxicological standards—primarily for air and food. See Herbert E. Stokinger and Richard L. Woodward, "Toxicologic Methods for Establishing Drinking Water Standards," *Journal, American Water Works Association,* Vol. 50, No. 4, April 1958, pp. 515 ff.

[45] Bernard B. Berger, Head of Water Supply and Water Pollution Research, Robert A. Taft Sanitary Engineering Center, USPHS, Cincinnati, Ohio, in conversation with the author.

[46] *Wall Street Journal,* February 10, 1961, p. 1. While these reported estimates may be exaggerated, the lower figure was also quoted to the author by Bernard B. Berger as an approximate minimum cost for testing the chronic toxicity of a single compound in water.

pound to undergo changes affecting its toxicity. Transformations of an analogous character have added appreciably to the air pollution problem.[47] In the notorious cranberry episode of 1960 the oxide of the herbicide heptachlore turned out to be much more toxic than the compound itself. In addition, the destructive effect of toxic chemicals ingested in combination apparently are ordinarily additive,[48] and in some instances synergistic or opposing. Consequently, there appears to be little immediate hope of obtaining reasonable tolerance standards for long-term ingestion of each of the many hundreds of toxic organic substances which, at least periodically, exist in waters drawn upon for public supplies.[49] Even if such standards could be elaborated, testing for each one would be an impossible burden for water utilities.

Actually, an analogous though much less extensive problem exists in regard to pathogenic organisms. In this case, the observation of coliform organisms is used as an indication of pathogens present. It has been suggested that a similarly simple index may be workable for organic chemicals.[50] This technique would be based upon the amount (in ppb) of organic materials that can be eluted from a carbon filter by repeated extractions with chloroform. The procedure is under consideration by the U.S. Public Health Service Advisory Committee on Revision of Drinking Water Standards. It appears likely that a limit of 200 ppb in finished water supplies will be recommended. Under current conditions this would not require special treatment of most public water supplies. The proposed concentration is based upon the fact that higher levels are usually associated with taste and odor problems. Theoretically, the specification of a limit based upon a composite measurement has many drawbacks, but its simplicity is appealing not only from the point of view of utility operation but also in terms of the amenability of pollution to cost analysis. The proposed aggregate standard provides a value

[47] Gordon M. Fair, "New Factors in Man's Management of his Environment," Chadwick Lecture delivered in the Royal Hall, Harrogate, on 28th of April, 1959, in conjunction with the Health Congress of the Royal Society of Health, pp. 11 ff.

[48] Herbert E. Stokinger and Richard L. Woodward, *op. cit.,* p. 528.

[49] Illustrative of the present degree of ignorance concerning the long-term effect of pollutants is the following comment by Professor H. J. Muller, "The production of mutations by chemicals, to some of which man is now exposed as a result of his own technology, has been known for two decades. It is a sad commentary on our culture, however, that there has been virtually no research on the extent to which mutations are actually being produced in this way in man or related animals by chemicals in the concentrations and under the conditions now existing in man's environment." Quotation from a letter to the author from Dr. Muller, Professor of Genetics, Indiana University.

[50] M. B. Ettinger, *op. cit.*

that could initially be inserted into such an analysis as a constraint. The recommended limit for finished water cannot be literally transposed to the raw water supply because the quantity of chloroform extractables can be somewhat altered by the utility operator. Thus, the use of activated carbon (see Chapter II) might be substituted for high-quality raw water over a limited range. This is particularly important because some of the organic chemicals are of diffuse origin and, consequently, expensive or impossible to segregate and dispose of at the source. Another possible method of reducing organic chemicals is the treatment of effluents or water supplies by means of artificial frothing.[51] On the other hand, the cost of using "soft" organics for purposes that contribute appreciably to organic pollution loads, and the cost of alternative nonchemical means of insect and herbal control, should be weighed against increased treatment costs.

In general, very little is known about the relative costs of these various methods, and the strong vested interests involved may well inhibit their objective investigation. However, the amount of organic chemicals found in raw water supplies (and finished water) is mounting rapidly, and society may soon choose to set drinking and stream water standards that require the elimination of substantial amounts of these substances.[52] Thus they may well assume a prominent role in any program for the optimum disposal of wastes. Unbiased natural and social science study of the range of alternatives available is badly needed.

In large measure the problem presently posed by the persistent chemicals is one of risk and uncertainty. Serious difficulties are involved in discovering the risk preferences of individuals and applying them in empirical formulations,[53] but it is clear that rational social decisions must include such considerations. Where probabilities can be clearly specified, as in the case of infectious disease, something like a social consensus may be discernible.

[51] A review of the literature on frothing methods and some new research results are reported in I. A. Eldib, "Foam Fractionation for Removal of Soluble Organics from Wastewater," *Journal, Water Pollution Control Federation,* September 1961, p. 914.

[52] For opposing views concerning the significance of the new organic pesticides, see the papers by Cottam and Hoffman in the section "Effects of Pesticides on Aquatic Life," *Biological Problems in Water Pollution, Transactions of the 1959 Seminar, op. cit.*

[53] Otto Eckstein, "A Survey of the Theory of Public Expenditure Criteria," in *Public Finances: Needs, Sources and Utilization,* a Conference of the Universities —National Bureau Committee for Economic Research (Princeton: Princeton University Press, 1961).

Particularly difficult problems of choice present themselves in regard to synthetic organics and radiological pollution, since their possible chronic effects are not known. In other words, there is no firm knowledge concerning the ill effects associated with various degrees of contamination even on a probability basis. In cases of uncertainty, no agreed-upon rational grounds for decision exist. However, methods of improving decisions can perhaps be found. For example, it may be possible to compute the cost of wholly or partially compensating for ignorance. This kind of calculation may be a highly significant aid in indicating the importance of research to remove ignorance in specific areas. In addition, specification of the costs of avoiding uncertain results permits society to play the game knowing at least part of the stakes. As has been previously indicated, one of the major virtues of the framework outlined in Part I is that it is conducive to examination of the cost implications of policy constraints.

Decisions in many fields, including medicine and health, are frequently made as though they were purely technical, when in fact they are a reflection of values.[54] Studies aimed at uncovering implicit value judgments, at explicitly stating probabilities, at attempting to discern social responses to risks and risk preference, at determining the precision with which the political process can be made to reflect social preferences, and at applying the best available decision tools are of high importance. As population density and urbanization increase and as technology changes, more or less pervasive changes in the physical environment will with increasing frequency confront society with difficult decisions in regard to public health.[55]

[54] For a good discussion of some value problems encountered in medicine, see René J. Dubos (Member and professor of the Rockefeller Institute), address before *The Dartmouth Convocation on Great Issues of Conscience in Modern Medicine,* September 8, 9, 10, 1960.

[55] Problems of risk and uncertainty are by no means limited to matters of public health insofar as pollution control planning is concerned. There are unavoidable elements of uncertainty in economic projections, and the dependence of pollution damages upon hydrology introduces an important element of risk.

VII

Problems in Devising Procedures for Approximating Optimum Systems

The conceptual, mathematical and computational problems involved in determining an optimum design for a system with the complexities of a multipurpose, multi-unit water resources development present a great challenge in themselves, disregarding data deficiencies. A distinction should be made between the "conventional" methods that have been applied to problems of this character by government agencies and the formal model solution, which is aimed at approximating the optimum system. The optimum system is the one that best fulfills the objective given the constraints—the one, for example, that minimizes the costs associated with waste disposal.

"Conventional" methods have several shortcomings: the consideration of comparatively few alternatives; design aimed at achieving physical objectives; and/or the application of rules of thumb when explicitly economic variables are relevant. An example of the latter is the use of minimum deficits of water for certain system purposes or, in the case of pollution, the use of a conventional design flow. The application of rules of thumb and the economic investigation of only small numbers of alternatives largely arise from the extensive data requirements and the complexity and difficulty of conceptually more satisfactory methods.

One may suppose that even comparatively crude methods of economic analysis can make a substantial contribution to improved decisions with respect to pollution control as additional information on physical and biological relationships and on costs becomes available. This is especially likely if such information is incorporated into planning that recognizes that pollution presents a problem of designing a system of interdependent units to achieve certain social goals. However, the increasingly complex and pressing character of water pollution problems emphasizes the desirability of developing methods that can rapidly deal with numerous variables and constraints and consequently help to select a system from among great numbers of possible alternatives. Special emphasis is added to this point by the desirability of investigating the costs and cost sensitivity of politically determined constraints. In recent years several students of multipurpose resources development have proposed, and at least partially explored, such methods,[1] but there have been no attempts to include water quality as a variable in them.[2]

POSSIBLE APPROACHES

The most fruitful approach to the discovery of optimum waste disposal system designs would have to be worked out over a period of time by persons possessing a variety of skills. The following exposition is meant only to convey an impression of the form such investigations might take and incidentally to highlight a few of the special problems likely to be encountered in formulating and solving system design models for waste disposal.

An initial step in working out a method, or methods, for solution might be to take a highly simplified situation and deal with it in terms of both physical and economic factors and the objective sought. A prototype basin might be utilized having a simple hydrology, comparatively few sources and types of pollution, relatively few water supply intakes, and a limited array of potential treatment and abatement measures. Also, only a small number of constraints representing aesthetic, recreational, and public health values might initially be incorporated. The character of these constraints would depend upon initial specification

---

[1] See for example, Earl O. Heady, "Mathematical Analysis Models for Quantitative Application in Watershed Planning," *Economics of Watershed Planning,* edited by G. S. Tolley and F. E. Riggs (Ames: The Iowa State University Press, 1961), and in the same volume Robert Dorfman, "Mathematical Analysis-Design of the Simple Valley Project." A general outline of the first two years of work of the Harvard Water Resources Seminar is found in Arthur Maass and Maynard M. Hufschmidt, "Report on the Harvard Program of Research in Water Resources Development," *Resources Development, Frontiers for Research* (Boulder: University of Colorado Press, 1960). Much of the discussion of this section is based upon the Maass-Hufschmidt presentation and conversation with Maynard Hufschmidt and Harold Thomas. A volume detailing the work of the seminar, *Design of Water Resources Systems,* is scheduled for publication by Harvard University Press, early in 1962.

[2] However, one effort of this character is planned by Harold Thomas and Associates at Harvard.

of the major uses of the receiving water and upon an initial judgment regarding design flow.

With respect to objectives sought, a first approach might be to attempt to minimize costs associated with the disposition of a predetermined quantity of wastes stemming from a specified population and from given industrial processes. This would mean minimizing the sum of all treatment (including water supply) costs, other abatement costs, and damages, subject to the constraints representing stream and water supply standards. Also, since the basin or the watershed is inevitably a somewhat arbitrary unit of analysis, some explicit assumption concerning terminal values of quality characteristics where the stream enters another stream or an estuary would be necessary. Not only may terminal values of certain pollutants be significant considerations, but some methods of coping with pollution that may be efficient cannot be considered without going beyond the bounds of the basin, i.e., interbasin transfers of water. This emphasizes the necessity of devoting analysis and judgment to selecting the area analyzed when an actual design problem is addressed.

In order to further avoid complications, which would exist in actual situations, it might be assumed in initial efforts that there are no impoundments on the stream or that the operating procedures of existing impoundments are not subject to change. Along the same line, it might be assumed that opportunities for low-flow augmentation would be single purpose in character. If these assumptions were not made, it would be necessary to consider the possibility of altering operating procedures of existing structures and to consider complementary and competitive relations between flow augmentation and other multiple-purpose flow regulation functions of new impoundments. The actual simplifications necessary to carry out an initial effort would have to be worked out in detail and would depend in considerable measure on the resources available to the investigators.

Previous efforts aimed at devising optimal system designs for water resources projects suggest that application of simulation or adaptions of mathematical programming techniques would yield promising results once the objective function, constraints, physical and economic relations, and parameters have been determined (or, for purpose of devising the model and its solution, assumed).[3]

Actually neither of these methods is the one likely to be intuitively most attractive to economists. Economists generally think in terms of

[3] See footnote 1 this chapter.

marginal relationships and incremental changes. However, marginal and other closely related methods have several weaknesses in problems of the type under consideration here.[4] Perhaps the most important is that the computations become very extensive when numerous variables and constraints are involved.[5]

Regardless of the method of solution, the optimum system must be one in which no marginal change can improve the situation. With respect to the cost minimization objective, this means that no marginal adjustment can cause over-all costs associated with waste disposal to fall and still permit the specified constraints to be met. Consequently the marginal method may be a useful supplement to other methods after they have identified a design near the optimum.

SIMULATION AND PROGRAMMING

Simulation is a very flexible method and can be used as an aid to planning in various ways. One way is as an element in a strategy which permits convergence on an optimal system design. In applying simulation the significant elements of a process are translated into a set of status variables, input variables, output variables, and relations. These elements are combined into a model, usually initially stated in mathematical form, which can be used to test the implications for, say, the output variables of a change in the input variables, in the relations of one component to another, or in the initial status of the system. Simulation of a pollution problem would, for example, view abatement measures and their related cost as inputs and reduction of pollution, with its related reduction of damages or contribution toward meeting the constraints, as outputs. By varying the inputs (dam sizes, capacity of lagoons, capacity of treatment plants,[6] operating procedures, etc.), the

---

[4] In practice, continuous derivatives must be approximated by finite differences.

[5] See Maass and Hufschmidt, *op. cit.*, for a further discussion of this technique. See also Stefan Valavanis, "Marginalism vs. Algorithmism," *Review of Economics and Statistics,* August 1958. See also the appendix by Alain C. Enthoven, "The Simple Mathematics of Maximization," in Charles J. Hitch and Roland N. McKean, *The Economics of Defense in the Nuclear Age* (Cambridge: Harvard University Press, 1960), for an excellent discussion of marginal conditions and the maximization process.

[6] Treatment is ordinarily thought of not as being continuously variable but as proceeding by stages—primary, secondary, tertiary—but there does not seem to be any substantial obstacle to varying it continuously. As an obvious example, it is possible to vary in a continuous fashion the portion of the effluent given treatment.

impact of different alternatives on total costs may be tested, say, for the known hydrological record. The results of each of these "runs" may be thought of as ". . . an experiment performed upon the model."[7] The results of a single run are specific and provide no evidence concerning efficiency. Indeed the results of a single run may be highly inefficient and in violation of the constraints. If the model is programmed for computer use, which would be the only practical procedure, a great number of "runs" can be made very quickly and those that violate constraints, or are inefficient, can be eliminated. By making numerous runs and applying sampling techniques, a constrained optimum (or in the present case, lowest cost) system design can be approached. The closeness of the approach is limited by the range of alternatives and operating procedures programmed into the machine and by the limitations of the sampling procedure. Random sampling of "runs," however, has a particularly attractive feature in that it permits probability statements to be made about the results.[8]

As explained previously, the analysis of pollution in isolation, while possibly useful in initial applications of methodology, is an unsatisfactory method for use in actual situations since it neglects important interdependencies in the use and control of water resources. There does not appear to be any conceptual reason why a simulation procedure could not include all aspects of multipurpose development. The obstacles lie largely in contriving and programming a model and in selecting from the numerous possible operating procedures which might be devised. The latter unfortunately are not generated by the machine in a simulation problem but must be given to it.

A very substantial advantage of simulation is its flexibility and adaptability. Its greatest disadvantage is that it does not automatically provide a procedure for converging on an optimal solution.

Mathematical programming techniques recommend themselves as an alternative to simulation for solving models because they are well adapted to problems involving a number of linear constraints and, under appropriate circumstances, they are capable of proceeding directly to the goal of optimum decisions, given a constrained objective function. In the case of basin-wide water resources planning, this means that they hold out the hope of simultaneously determining optimum combina-

---

[7] See Guy H. Orcutt, "Simulation of Economic Systems," *The American Economic Review,* December 1960.

[8] See Maass and Hufschmidt, *op. cit.,* for a discussion of alternative sampling methods, some of their merits and demerits, and the benefits of using them in combination.

tions of structures and optimum operating procedures at least to a first approximation. Also, the setup of a linear programming problem is such that it can automatically incorporate economic values as an integral part of the iterative process leading to the determination of an optimal feasible program.[9]

Among the most difficult obstacles confronting efforts to apply programming techniques to water resources planning have been nonlinearities in input-output relationships and the incorporation of "probability" elements into the program.[10] These elements are an essential part of basin planning problems because of the crucial role played by hydrology,[11] and nonlinearities resulting from diminishing marginal rates of substitution are probably fairly common in production including

[9] The significance of the introduction of economic values as an integral part of the planning process may not be immediately apparent. If a given type of productive facility produces only one type of output, the specification of maximum output, given the inputs, is a purely physical problem. There will be one way, and only one way, to combine the inputs in order to produce maximum output. If the price per unit of the output is also given, solution of the physical maximization problem will also produce maximum value of output given the inputs. But, in the case of multiple outputs, the maximum value of output cannot be found based upon a physical maximization procedure, even if the price of the outputs is specified. It is still possible to find the maximum output of one product, *given* the level of the others, solely on the basis of physical considerations. However, to find the maximum *value* of output, it is necessary to consider the relative value of the several outputs. In many situations, when inputs are given, the value of one output can be increased only at the expense of other outputs, i.e., they are substitutes in production. Thus the appropriate manner of using and combining the inputs becomes a problem in resources allocation which can be solved only by giving co-ordinate consideration to technical relationships and economic values. A highly simplified example of what this means in regard to water resources planning may be helpful. Suppose a basin having development opportunities for two dam sites is suitable only for the production of electric power. Given an arbitrary size of the two dams and their generating plants, the basin hydrology, and the price of electricity, the operating procedure which yields the maximum value of output over a given period of time can be specified on purely technical grounds. The specified output may not be optimum in the sense of maximizing the difference between revenues and costs, but it will be the most that can be obtained under the circumstances. However, if irrigation is introduced into the system, finding a point that maximizes the value of output given the dam sizes requires the consideration of economic values. Thus, in system planning, the specification of alternatives on the basis of physical maximization of only one of the outputs and the subsequent application of values neglects an important part of the economic maximization problem.

[10] One advantage of the simulation approach is that it does not require linear functions. See Kalman J. Cohen and Richard M. Cyert, "Computer Models—Dynamic Economics," *Quarterly Journal of Economics*, February 1961, p. 112.

[11] Risks and uncertainties enter in many other connections, some of which are mentioned elsewhere.

some of the processes resulting in water derivative goods and those used in water treatment. Furthermore, if the area being analyzed is comparatively large (say, a basin), price may not be independent of production, and marginal value productivities as well as marginal costs of acquiring inputs may be influenced by the scale of production.

Price variation can be avoided by dealing with relatively small areas, but nonlinearity in input-output relationships probably can not. The latter difficulty can be dealt with by defining a number of vectors and activities for each product, which can then be treated as a production function composed of linear segments. Other approaches have also been outlined including some able to deal with simple price output dependency relationships.[12] Also, promising steps toward introducing stochastic elements into the mathematical programming of water resources development systems have been made.[13] All of these extensions and modifications of the basic model add to computational complexities. One question which research must answer is whether a fairly detailed treatment of an actual multipurpose multi-unit basin development incorporating stochastic elements and some nonlinearities exceeds the bounds of even potential computational feasibility.

While application of programming has thus far been to comparatively simple situations, experimentation aimed at evaluating its application to the design problems of a waste-disposal system seems merited.

PROBLEMS OF TIMING AND SEQUENCE

Pressures on the load carrying of some rivers in the future may require the utilization of comparatively formal techniques to co-ordinate loadings with capacity in a manner consistent with the multiple function of water courses. When wastes are discharged into a stream they

[12] See references in Heady, *op. cit.,* p. 22. Even cases of decreasing cost, which are probably relevant to basin planning problems, may be amenable of solution using programming techniques. Harry Markowitz and Alan S. Manne, "On the Solution of Discrete Programming Problems," *Econometrica,* Vol. 25, January 1957. This method results in difficulties in the interpretation of the "duals," however. Ralph E. Gomorzy and William Baumol, "Integer Programming and Pricing," *Econometrica,* Vol. 28, July 1960.

[13] See Maass and Hufschmidt, *op. cit.,* p. 176. Further information on development in the handling of time, nonlinearities and stochastic elements in programming solutions to water resources system design will be found in *Design of Water Resources Systems,* to be published by the Harvard University Press in 1962.

may or may not mix uniformly with the water passing the outfall during the period of discharge. Regardless of the degree of lateral mixing, however, the wastes tend to travel downstream with that portion of the stream into which they were discharged. Thus, for example, a plant which discharges during working hours but not at night gives rise to surges of pollution. In the case of some pollutants and under some stream conditions these surges will persist far downstream. Various problems may arise from this tendency for pollutants to pass downstream in a body. For example, plant A discharges chlorides (highly persistent) for twelve hours a day. Plant B, located twelve hours downstream, also discharges chlorides for twelve hours a day. Plant B discharge begins just as Plant A's slug arrives, possibly giving rise to damaging chloride concentrations downstream. Another example: Coal field A operates its pumps only during working hours, giving rise to diurnal peaks of acidity in the stream. These coincide with the discharges of hexavalent chromium or other toxins downstream, thus greatly increasing the toxicity of the effluent to fish. In practice, the interrelationships of various polluters along a stream are much more complex than the above situations would suggest and are seldom known in any detail. The types of co-ordination problems which may arise are in some respects similar to those dealt with in queing and inventory theory. It appears possible that these or other techniques in the general area of operations research would be found useful in the analysis of pollution problems in particular stretches of streams, aside from the part they might play in over-all basin planning.

CONCLUDING COMMENTS

The amount of investment that will be required in pollution control in the next several decades makes it important that the most effective methods be applied to the efficient attainment of objectives in the field. Experimentation to establish applicability of formal systems analysis techniques to pollution problems, and to include water quality in the general problem of efficient water resource systems design is highly important in this regard.

It is worth repeating that decision models (utilizing a constrained objective function) and appropriate means of solving them are adaptable to a wide variety of goals, and to a limited degree to the analysis

of constraints. Indeed, one of the most important contributions of
these procedures might be in performing the kinds of "experiments"
on constraints and design-flows outlined in Part I. If a successful programming approach were devised, the "dual" of the solution would provide interesting information in this respect since it imputes marginal
values to the effective constraints. Similarly, simulation could be used
to test the cost sensitivity of the constraints by successive optimizing
simulation procedures each using a different value for a constraint.

Research directed toward the use of systems analysis techniques
with respect to pollution problems might also make a significant contribution to the planning process in complex metropolitan areas containing numerous municipalities and residential areas with separate
sewage systems. Even though sewage disposal may be the single most
significant element determining the ability of water resources in an
area to support economic and demographic growth and furnish amenities, it apparently is seldom explicitly viewed as part of a comprehensive
plan for area development. Almost any sanitary engineer can recount
instances of undesirable results stemming from the insufficient planning
of sewage disposal systems. Obviously, however, engineering or technical decisions cannot be the determining elements in such planning.
The problem has recently been well stated as follows:

> Present sewage disposal systems have largely resulted from single
> focus technical-engineering studies. When performed in isolation,
> without consideration of other important community needs and prob-
> lems, such technical analysis automatically "makes," through default,
> decisions which go far beyond sewerage facility and concern and affect
> the future of the entire community and sometimes entire watersheds.
> Such automatic "decisions" occur during technical elaboration of
> quantified assumptions about future "needs" when these are derived
> from single perspectives unrelated to other controlling or influencing
> factors.[14]

Adequate regional planning would have to consider alternative systems of disposal (not only combinations of units but such matters as
design-flows) in the context of over-all factors entering into the attainment of objectives. Such studies not only require skill but present difficult problems of calculation and judgment. Projects of this kind should
comprehend the skills of several professional fields as well as specialized

[14] Sanford S. Farness (Director, Tri-County Regional Planning Commission),
"Some Comments on Present Sewage Disposal and River Use Problems and
Programs in the Lansing Area," April 1960. Mimeo.

and sophisticated means of analysis. The application of operations research techniques merits testing, and, for the more comprehensive planning problems discussed earlier, means for efficient computation of the impact upon receiving waters of alternative waste-disposal systems are needed.[15]

Finally, it must be said that the application of systems analysis techniques to pollution control and, even more, to the full scope of system design is an exceedingly complex difficult task and is unlikely to lead to fully dependable solutions. Despite the best efforts of skilled researchers, much of the required information will continue to be less than ideal in form and dependability. Moreover, as indicated in the previous chapter, an unavoidable amount of uncertainty will always afflict the decision-making process. Consequently, considerable regard must be given to the virtues of flexibility and adaptability when pollution control plans are devised. One of the important questions which research must answer is the extent to which complex techniques can be carried and still yield a positive return in terms of improved decisions and/or an improved method of making decisions. Certainly, one of the marginal costs which should not be neglected is the marginal cost of making marginal refinements.

---

[15] The computational burdens involved in testing alternative plant sizes, design flows, and stream standards are sufficiently large to seriously circumscribe the consideration of many alternative situations even in respect to the design of a plant for a single outfall. The use of electronic computers in this field has barely begun to develop.

VIII

Summary of Part I and a Brief Review of Selected Research Needs

SUMMARY OF PART I

The results of unregulated waste disposal into bodies of water fail to coincide with the attributes of an ideally functioning market system. To an extent these failures can be attributed to pollution-established links between fiscally independent economic units. Such links (external diseconomies) result in inefficient waste-disposal systems, in excessive waste disposal, and in a non-optimal distribution of social costs.

It was suggested that a reasonable, broad goal of public policy would be to minimize the social costs associated with waste disposal. This implies, among other things, that a public authority would take account of the effects of waste disposal that are external to the individual economic units and that affect water quality within a relevant area—say a basin. Typically such an area would contain numerous separately managed waste sources, water supply intakes, publicly and privately used intervening stretches of stream and shoreline and, in some instances, navigation facilities and flow regulation devices as well.

If markets operate in such a way that market prices can be viewed as reasonable approximations to social costs and benefits, minimization of social waste disposal costs implies a policy which equalizes in all directions the marginal costs associated with waste disposal. These costs include not only the direct costs of sewage treatment, flow-augmentation, holding lagoons, reregulation, etc., but the marginal damages or costs imposed on other water uses as well. The latter include water-supply treatment stemming from pollution, damages to all sorts of facilities, and the reduced value of non-diversion uses such as navigation, commercial fisheries, recreation, etc. An optimal system designed to achieve the stated objective would probably permit some pollution, albeit less than if the market were operating in an uninhibited fashion.

96

Pollution poses a problem in designing an efficient, interdependent system of waste disposal, one in which social cost is held to a minimum. Recognition of this fact was proposed as a reasonable point of departure for public policy, but some complications were noted. Conditions of consumption and of supply can be such that individual market valuations either do not exist and cannot be imputed, or, if available, do not yield the appropriate social valuation. General environmental qualities and public health are such instances. The former is an instance where conditions of supply make it impossible for similarly situated individuals to consume a service in different amounts and therefore prevent the development of a market that would register individual preferences. Public health is an example of interdependency in consumption, which prevents parity between private and social preferences. Moreover, in the case of some destructive aspects of pollution, inability to determine a market-type valuation based on individual willingness to pay, might arise more from measurement problems than from the inherent character of the good or service. Recreation is in this category.

Where market-type valuations are not feasible or meaningful, political valuations, which admit explicitly collective considerations, were said to be implied in a democratic system. It was suggested that public authorities could introduce "public" values or goals by setting standards that would limit, or constrain, the general cost minimization objective. The costs of the constraints, in terms of the objectives, could be determined, and this would provide a measure of what the conditions they specify (say, maintenance of aerobic conditions) must "at least" be worth. Furthermore, the cost sensitivity of the constraints could be tested by determining a range of optimal system designs, each with different levels of constraints. This would be one means of providing public decision makers with information permitting them to make informed judgments concerning the preferences of society.

A further complication for a policy of minimizing the social costs of waste disposal arises from the complementary and competitive relationships between waste dilution and other aspects of multipurpose river valley development. This means that the design of optimal waste-disposal systems is inherently a part of the general problem of designing and executing optimum multipurpose water resources development programs. This, in turn, implies that public planning authorities ideally should consider all alternative water uses (including waste dilution), the effects on quality of the various uses, the losses imposed on other uses by quality deterioration, and the value of all relevant water uses.

Ideally, they should consider all feasible alternative system designs and operating procedures and derive a solution which indicates the optimum combination of system elements and operating procedures. Unless this is done, the costs (including damages and the value of foregone opportunities) associated with disposal of the wastes generated in a basin cannot be minimized.

Stating the problem in this idealized form was not meant to imply that fully optimum systems are an immediately realistic objective, but to point up the types of information that can improve social decisions with respect to water pollution control. Explicit treatment of water pollution as a problem in system design and improved information on physical, biological, and cost aspects will contribute to this objective even though ideal data and analytic methods are not immediately realizable.

RESEARCH NEEDS

The types of improved scientific understanding, increases in data, and methodological improvements implied by the policy framework developed in Part I may be put into five categories:

(a) Information on what happens to wastes in receiving water and their effects on the water, particularly wastes that cause tangible changes in the water itself or significantly affect successive uses.

(b) A methodology for keeping track of quality changes and quickly computing the concentration of pollutants (and significant associated variables such as D.O.) at all relevant points of use, as a function of a variety of conditioning factors. The latter include waste loads at particular outfalls, biological, chemical, and physical conditions, and volume of stream flow.

(c) Information on the costs of waste disposal. These include sewage treatment, water-supply treatment, reclamation of waste materials, industrial process changes, methods of controlling stream flow or conforming waste discharges to flows, and pollution damages (including those that occur indirectly, say, as a consequence of algae growth).

(d) Improved means for the prediction of pollution loadings—especially those resulting from industrial waste disposal. These should provide a reasonable forecast of the effects of environmental conditions such as water costs, technological changes, and various kinds of public policies.

(e) Improved techniques for approximating optimum multipurpose multi-unit system designs when the objective is constrained in various ways. These techniques should be capable of handling the many complexities introduced when waste disposal, and attendant water quality variation, is included in the design problem.

Physical and Biological Research and Methods of Forecasting Pollution Effects on Streams

Work is now under way in universities, government, and industry bearing upon the needs in the indicated areas and efforts have been initiated toward producing a computer program to meet the need stated in category (b). Moreover, category (a) has long been a matter of central interest to sanitary engineering and related scientific research, and much is known about the extraordinarily complex phenomena that occur in bodies of water. However, there are still substantial gaps, and much of what is known needs to be organized in a fashion more suitable for the analysis of pollution as a problem in designing efficient waste-disposal systems.

Although there has been some study of phenomena of a broader character, the traditional focus of sanitary engineering has been upon effects traceable to particular waste outfalls over limited stretches of stream. Some of the most important challenges to physical and biological research concern the plant nutrient, algae growth, photosynthetic oxygen complex of effects in receiving water. Especially challenging are the indirect and long-delayed effects that are modified substantially but in currently imperfectly predictable ways by the receiving water environment itself. These problems of broad significance bear not only upon the accurate computation of waste assimilation in the receiving water but upon such matters as the comparability of results of waste treatment by stabilization ponds and other methods. Some of the most difficult unresolved questions of this type occur with respect to lakes, estuaries, and impoundments. Other aspects of oxygen balance such as the effects of various industrial and domestic pollutants on BOD and reaeration through the interface are insufficiently well understood. Among the approaches that merit investigation are behavioristic ones depending upon multivariate statistical analysis.

Accurate prediction of the direct and indirect effects of given amounts and types of pollutants on receiving waters is fundamental to any rational, comprehensive, pollution-control planning effort. Greater research in this highly complex field is definitely merited. As the effort to devise a model for the prediction of pollution concentrations proceeds, a major benefit should be further identification of critical problem areas, especially when predictions are tested in actual streams.

Pollution Costs, Projections of Pollution Loadings, and Optimal System Design

Since there has been practically no rigorous analysis of costs from the point of view of designing efficient, interdependent systems, remarkably little is known about how various treatment devices, alternative means of water-quality control, and pollution damages substitute for one another under various conditions, i.e., how they would tend to combine into optimum systems. Moreover, the forecasting of pollution loadings is in its infancy. Little or nothing is known about a number of critical relationships—especially with respect to industrial waste loads. It is in regard to research on costs and optimal design, and factors underlying the generation of wastes, that the social sciences, working with sanitary engineering and related scientific disciplines, may be expected to make their major contribution.[1] In the following pages a group of research needs in these areas, selected from the discussion of Chapters VI and VII, is briefly reviewed.

Industry. Industry is currently responsible for perhaps half the total degradable organic pollution load and a much larger share of inorganic and persistent organics, and heat, but comparatively little is known about its present and prospective role in the social costs of pollution. For example, no detailed comprehensive information is available concerning the pollution loads of various industries and how and at what cost they may be altered by process changes such as recirculation of water, or materials saving adjustments. Nor is much available about such matters as pollution damages to industrial equipment, industrial water-treatment costs, and the costs of treatment of

---

[1] The major focus of RFF's research interest is upon those areas where the social sciences, or social and physical sciences working together, can make a contribution to constructive pollution control policy and practice. Consequently, somewhat more extensive discussion is devoted to a *selected* group of these than to the more straightforwardly physical and biological research needs indicated in categories 1 and 2 of the above listing.

various types of industrial wastes (all as functions of relevant water and waste-water variables), even though these represent some of the more clear-cut social costs of waste disposal. Studies focused specifically upon each of the major water-using polluting industries, co-operatively carried out by engineers and economists, would be a logical approach toward expanding knowledge in appropriate directions. These studies should include both historical and cross-section analysis. Because of the interrelations between industrial locations, water supply, water depletion, and waste-water disposal, the studies should comprehend the over-all effect on, and responses to, the water resources environment. In addition to providing information on current cost relationships, such studies should yield useful knowledge for the projection of national and regional waste loadings, and the comparative costs of control devices, such as temporary lagooning, whose main promise appears to be in industrial applications.

Among the industries that merit specific investigation are: food and kindred products, pulp and paper, petroleum and products, iron and steel, textiles, rubber and products, and chemicals groups. Steam electric power generation, which produces large amounts of waste heat, should also be studied in the manner previously outlined. These investigations are of the first order of importance because industrial wastes are a very large and potentially variable part of the total wastes delivered to receiving waters. Projections of potential waste loads and knowledge of relevant types of industrial waste disposal and water costs are a necessary element in any rational, comprehensive, waste-disposal planning, whether it incorporates formal optimization procedures or not.

Sewage and Water Treatment. The character of the variation of cost with size of installations is critical in planning efficient waste-disposal systems. While some scattered and partial information exists, detailed studies of costs and cost variation in sewage and water treatment plants remain to be made.

These studies should be approached as industrial plants with a number of inputs (including water and waste water of various qualities), and both records of actual operation and engineering estimates of input-output relationships should be used. With respect to sewage treatment, the studies should analyze primary treatment and major types of secondary treatment separately (as functions of size and quality of output), so that costs of combining the two in various proportions can be inferred. Not only incremental cost estimates for planning treatment plants, but also estimates of cost variation in correspondence with differing operating procedures of given plants should be studied. Economies realizable by adjusting sewage plant operation to flow variations and other stream water quality changes should be studied, as should cost aspects of alterations in water-treatment plant operating procedures to conform with variations in intake water quality. If possible, these studies should incorporate an evaluation of the automatic monitoring equipment which is presently being used on an experimental basis in the Delaware and Ohio basins.

Because a major portion of the future costs of waste-disposal systems will undoubtedly be for sewage and water-supply treatment plants, it is important to have studies that help to forecast costs accurately and efficient means for incorporation of these plants into optimal systems.

Damages to Facilities and Costs Imposed by Municipal Water Supplies. While private incentives can probably be relied upon to achieve near-optimal relationships between industrial water-supply treatment and residual damages or other increased costs, the same is not true of public supplies. The relationship between water treatment costs, damages to facilities, and other costs imposed upon municipal users, is therefore a matter for public policy. These damages and imposed costs include corrosion of equipment, scale formation, increased soap usage, outlays for water softeners and bottled water, and a variety of others. The intimate relationship of public water supplies to public health and the conflicting needs of different consumers make the determination of optimal relationships between treatment and other costs particularly difficult. However, the more tangible costs of different qualities of public supplies must be considered in defining optimal systems even where public health effects cannot be evaluated in fully comparable terms. Moreover, a number of quality characteristics that may impose substantial costs have, within usual limits, little to do with public health. Consequently a systematic study of *net* costs, taking into consideration both the costs and gains resulting from certain quality changes (hardness, acidity, alkalinity, chlorides, temperature, tastes and odors, for example), would supply significant information for public planning.

Studies of this kind should identify the major factors that may cause costs to vary with the location and size of cities. Case studies of several cities might be useful. Effects traceable to pollution loadings should be isolated from those due to natural quality characteristics of the water.

Recreation. Some of the costs of pollution that are the most difficult to value are also among the most important. Certain types of recreation, for example, impose unusually high quality requirements. Water-based recreation will be among the more important determinants of the level at which pollution abatement programs are conducted, in part because water-supply treatment and related measures cannot be substituted for pollution control. An effort to determine market-type valuations of the social costs imposed by destruction of recreation opportunities has been under way at RFF for the past several years with some interesting preliminary results. However, additional studies are in order, and special attention should be given to identifying demands for separate categories of water-based recreation such as fishing, swimming, and boating. The nature of pollution is such that opportunities for one or more of these forms of recreation can often be preserved while others are destroyed.

Although a fully satisfactory method of projecting recreation demand is not yet at hand, several methods can at least partially evaluate recreation in waste-disposal systems. One way is the use of variable policy constraints together with calculations of what the value of their effects must "at least" be worth. Such an approach might be experimented with in the prototype or case studies suggested below. Furthermore, the efficacy of stream specialization (classification and zoning) as a tool for the provision of efficient waste-disposal programs should be investigated. *A priori,* there are reasons to suppose that social costs could be reduced by this device, but the question is complicated by the difficulties of measuring demand. One approach would be to investigate the comparative costs of maintaining recreation water quality at various levels for different streams or stretches of stream in a basin. Again, case studies of simple situations might be used to experiment with methodologies of the types indicated.

The striking rate of increase in outdoor recreation, the intimate relation of many outdoor recreation activities to water, and the high quality of stream and lake water needed for most of these activities, make improved means of direct or indirect social valuation among the most important research topics in the entire field of planning for socially efficient waste disposal. Among the important questions requiring study is the efficacy of the political process in expressing relative social values when prices or imputed values from market behavior prove unworkable or unsatisfactory.

Public Health. Public health presents a series of difficult and important but elusive problems that overlap political, economic, and technical areas. These include decisions that appear to be technical but actually imply social value judgments, problems of appropriate accounting for risks and uncertainty in the social decision-making process, and questions concerning the precision with which political processes can be used to make socially meaningful decisions about technically complex problems. Again, as with respect to recreation, experimentation with the cost of variable constraint levels will probably play a significant role in the approximation of socially optimal levels of water quality for public health purposes. Where uncertainty of effects is involved, the social decision process can be aided by calculations which shed light upon the cost of "compensating for ignorance." Studies on these matters should provide useful information for other areas where the political process must be called upon in implementing social choice.

Once maximum admissible (constraint) levels are set for substances affecting public health, economically interesting problems of suboptimization remain. These are particularly difficult with respect to synthetic organics because of the range of possible control measures about which, as yet, very little is known. These include the use of activated carbon, artificial frothing, selective organisms in treatment plants, "soft organics," industrial plant process changes, nonchemical means of insect and herbal control, and perhaps others. Much further physical, biological, and economic knowledge is required to identify and permit satisfactory evaluation of all potentially feasible alternatives. Careful disinterested study of alternatives is of particular importance because of the intense and powerful vested interests involved. In regard to designing an optimum system to meet public health, as well as other, goals, the identification and evaluation of all reasonable alternatives is highly important. It may be far more important than the adoption of a best procedure for analyzing an incomplete array of alternatives.

Fisheries and Agriculture. Damage to commercial fisheries can be a social cost of pollution but one that is very difficult to measure accurately. Moreover, the character of the *net* loss (value of catch lost minus value of transferable resources) has often been misunderstood. Difficulties of measurement result from the fact that gauging damages to commercial fisheries presents some of the most challenging technical problems in the pollution field. This is true in part because whatever damages may occur are usually in lakes, estuaries, and coastal waters where the effects of pollution are particularly difficult to trace, and in part because the effects of pollution are difficult to isolate from other changes that influence the quality of fishing. However, even though case studies would need to depend to a substantial degree upon conjecture, and consequently their results would not be ideal, they should suffice to shed some light on the degree to which net damages foregone could participate in the justification of abatement programs.

Recent decades have seen a strong movement of industry westward and a tendency for irrigation to spread eastward. Supplementary irrigation especially has grown rapidly in the Middle West and East. More conflicts arising from salinity problems and industrial waste disposal can be expected in the future, and in some instances agricultural considerations—including irrigation with sewage effluents—may be expected to play a significant part in the design of efficient waste-disposal systems. Systematic studies focused explicitly upon the present and prospective place of agriculture in pollution problems should provide systematic information on the effect of irrigation upon water quality and the costs imposed upon agriculture by industrial pollution of various kinds.

Areas More Appropriately Investigated in System Context. Thus far, problem areas have been divided along basically functional lines. It is felt that these areas might be fruitfully studied as individual projects or sets of projects, but always with a view to their interrelationship within a water resources *system.* This approach should yield knowledge of wide applicability.

However, some aspects of pollution control might better be studied within actual or prototype geographical areas. For example, such an approach would be suitable for providing useful knowledge concerning the role of measures such as flow augmentation, temporary lagooning of wastes, reregulation, and stabilization ponds in waste-disposal systems. This is not to suggest that more physical, biological, and economic knowledge about each of these measures is not necessary, or that the research suggested in earlier sections is not a prerequisite to fully satisfactory analysis of their place in an optimum system. It merely reflects the fact that the costs of these measures are more a function of their specific physical and economic environment than are those, for example, of sewage and water supply treatment. Their comparative costs depend, to an unusual degree, upon hydrology, land values, availability of reservoir sites, and, in the case of flow augmentation, the value of other competitive or complementary purposes. However, initial analysis would have to depend upon numerous (reasonable) assumptions or

crude data concerning necessary elements in the analysis of cost-minimizing designs until results are available from further research in a
variety of fields.

Several case studies of simple, actual, or realistic prototype areas,
displaying a variety of conditions of hydrology, population, industrial
distribution, climate and multipurpose development would be useful
in identifying feasible alternatives and evaluating their potential role in
pollution abatement planning. Studies of this type would also help to
indicate the sensitivity of the mix of system components, and their individual cost sensitivity, to differing conditions. Moreover, they would
provide indications concerning the way in which flow augmentation
"trades off" against other project purposes in multipurpose developments under various hydrologic, and other conditions. Studies of this
general character should also endeavor to reflect the comparative
advantage of harvested ponds as contrasted to dilution, land disposal,
or other measures, in dealing with plant nutrients. While their primary
objectives would be to yield necessary empirical relationships, the case
studies would also provide excellent opportunities for the development
and testing of optimizing procedures.

Similarly, a case study approach with respect to water resources
planning in complex metropolitan areas containing numerous municipalities, residential areas, and industrial developments, with separate sewage
and water supply systems, could be expected to yield interesting results.
Even though sewage disposal may be the single most significant element
determining the ability of water resources in an area to support economic
and demographic growth and furnish amenities, it apparently is seldom
explicitly viewed as part of a comprehensive plan for area development. Again, case studies of a metropolitan complex would provide
an opportunity for experimentation with formal optimizing procedures.

*Techniques for Approximating Optimum Multipurpose Multi-unit
Systems.* The efforts of the Harvard Water Resources Seminar and
other less comprehensive investigations have led to promising methodologies for discovering water resources system designs that best fulfill a
stated objective. However, these efforts have not yet included water
quality as a variable. Also, the actual solutions reported have dealt
with simplified prototype systems and have used a simple objective
function not incorporating social goals incommensurable with market
valuations.

It is important that work on applying systematic maximizing procedures to system design be continued and extended to actual design problems. Since water quality is likely to become one of the most important considerations in many future system designs, it is especially important that procedures be specifically adapted to handle the complexities of waste-disposal system design. Efforts to devise maximizing models and means of solution specifically comprehending water quality should be undertaken using assumed values and relationships where necessary.

Several ways of approaching such an undertaking suggest themselves, and alternative approaches should be tried. For example, an initial effort utilizing a prototype basin might be aimed at devising a comparatively gross model dealing simultaneously with a number of system purposes including waste disposal. Alternatively, a more detailed model, which structured the problem in such a way that methods for best fulfilling a (constrained) waste disposal cost minimization objective, could be investigated without simultaneously having to optimize for other system purposes.

Experimentation to establish and evaluate maximization methodology suitable for waste-disposal analysis in metropolitan as well as larger areas will gain in importance as water quality attains a (probably) dominant role in Eastern water resources development.

CONCLUDING STATEMENT

This study has shown that any effort to establish efficient water-supply and waste-disposal systems is bound to be beset by a host of informational deficiencies, which cut across the boundaries of a variety of traditional disciplines.

The objective has been to outline the characteristics of economically efficient systems and to identify some of the more critical improvements in knowledge necessary to approximate such systems. This was done without specifically confronting the range of relevant problems of an institutional and administrative character. It was felt that these could more fruitfully be approached once economic and technical aspects are better understood. A number of lines of investigation have been suggested which should help to pinpoint the costs of pollution and enhance methodology and knowledge of scientific relationships critical for dealing with present and emerging waste-disposal problems in a socially meaningful and economically efficient manner.